Get Your Hands on Clean Architecture

A hands-on guide to creating clean web applications with code examples in Java

Tom Hombergs

Get Your Hands Dirty on Clean Architecture

Author: Tom Hombergs

Managing Editor: Aditya Shah

Acquisitions Editor: Bridget Neale

Production Editor: Shantanu Zagade

Editorial Board: Shubhopriya Banerjee, Ewan Buckingham, Mahesh Dhyani, Taabish Khan, Manasa Kumar, Alex Mazonowicz, Pramod Menon, Bridget Neale, Dominic Pereira, Shiny Poojary, Erol Staveley, Ankita Thakur, Nitesh Thakur, and Jonathan Wray

First Published: September 2019

Production Reference: 1270919

ISBN: 978-1-83921-196-6

Published by Packt Publishing Ltd.

Livery Place, 35 Livery Street

Birmingham B3 2PB, UK

Table of Contents

Preface i

Chapter 1: What's Wrong with Layers?   1

It Promotes Database-Driven Design 2

It's Prone to Shortcuts 4

It Grows Hard to Test 5

It Hides the Use Cases 6

It Makes Parallel Work Difficult 7

How Does This Help Me Build Maintainable Software? 8

Chapter 2: Inverting Dependencies   11

The Single Responsibility Principle 11

A Tale about Side Effects 13

The Dependency Inversion Principle 13

Clean Architecture 14

Hexagonal Architecture 16

How Does This Help Me Build Maintainable Software? 18

Chapter 3: Organizing Code   21

Organizing by Layer 22

Organizing by Feature 23

An Architecturally Expressive Package Structure 24

The Role of Dependency Injection 26

How Does This Help Me Build Maintainable Software? 28

Chapter 4: Implementing a Use Case   31

Implementing the Domain Model 32

A Use Case in a Nutshell 34

Validating Input 36

The Power of Constructors 40

Different Input Models for Different Use Cases 41

Validating Business Rules 42

Rich versus Anemic Domain Model 44

Different Output Models for Different Use Cases 45

What about Read-Only Use Cases? 46

How Does This Help Me Build Maintainable Software? 47

Chapter 5: Implementing a Web Adapter   49

Dependency Inversion 50

Responsibilities of a Web Adapter 51

Slicing Controllers 53

How Does This Help Me Build Maintainable Software? 57

Chapter 6: Implementing a Persistence Adapter   59

Dependency Inversion 59

The Responsibilities of a Persistence Adapter 60

Slicing Port Interfaces 61

Slicing Persistence Adapters 63

Example with Spring Data JPA 65

What about Database Transactions? 72

How Does This Help Me Build Maintainable Software? 72

Chapter 7: Testing Architecture Elements   75

The Test Pyramid 76

Testing a Domain Entity with Unit Tests 77

Testing a Use Case with Unit Tests 78

Testing a Web Adapter with Integration Tests 80

Testing a Persistence Adapter with Integration Tests 82

Testing Main Paths with System Tests 85

How Much Testing is Enough? 88

How Does This Help Me Build Maintainable Software? 89

Chapter 8: Mapping Between Boundaries   91

The "No Mapping" Strategy 92

The "Two-Way" Mapping Strategy 93

The "Full" Mapping Strategy 95

The "One-Way" Mapping Strategy 96

When to Use Which Mapping Strategy? 97

How Does This Help Me Build Maintainable Software? 98

Chapter 9: Assembling the Application   101

Why Even Care about Assembly? 101

Assembling via Plain Code 103

Assembling via Spring's Classpath Scanning 105

Assembling via Spring's Java Config 107

How Does This Help Me Build Maintainable Software? 109

Chapter 10: Enforcing Architecture Boundaries   113

Boundaries and Dependencies 114

Visibility Modifiers 115

Post-Compile Checks 117

Build Artifacts 119

How Does This Help Me Build Maintainable Software? 123

Chapter 11: Taking Shortcuts Consciously   125

Why Shortcuts Are Like Broken Windows 125

The Responsibility of Starting Clean 127

Sharing Models between Use Cases 127

Using Domain Entities as Input or Output Models 129

Skipping Incoming Ports 130

Skipping Application Services 131

How Does This Help Me Build Maintainable Software? 132

Chapter 12: Deciding on an Architecture Style   135

The Domain is King 136

Experience is Queen 136

It Depends 137

Index   139

Preface

About

This section briefly introduces the author and the coverage of this book.

About the Book

We would all like to build software architecture that yields adaptable and flexible software with low development costs. But, unreasonable deadlines and shortcuts make it very hard to create such an architecture.

Get Your Hands Dirty on Clean Architecture starts with a discussion about the conventional layered architecture style and its disadvantages. It also talks about the advantages of the domain-centric architecture styles of Robert C. Martin's Clean Architecture and Alistair Cockburn's Hexagonal Architecture. Then, the book dives into hands-on chapters that show you how to manifest a hexagonal architecture in actual code. You'll learn in detail about different mapping strategies between the layers of a hexagonal architecture and see how to assemble the architecture elements into an application. The later chapters demonstrate how to enforce architecture boundaries. You'll also learn what shortcuts produce what types of technical debt and how, sometimes, it is a good idea to willingly take on those debts.

After reading this book, you'll have all the knowledge you need to create applications using the hexagonal architecture style of web development.

About the Author

Tom Hombergs is a software engineer by profession and by passion with more than a decade of experience working on many different software projects for many different clients across various industries. In software projects, he takes on the roles of software developer, architect, and coach, with a focus on the Java ecosystem. He has found that writing is the best way to learn, so he likes to dive deep into topics he encounters in his software projects to create texts that give structure to the chaotic world of software development. He regularly writes about software development on his blog at reflectoring.io and is an occasional speaker at conferences.

Learning Objectives

By the end of this course, you will be able to:

- Identify potential shortcomings of using a layered architecture
- Apply methods to enforce architecture boundaries
- Find out how potential shortcuts can affect the software architecture
- Produce arguments for when to use which style of architecture
- Structure your code according to the architecture
- Apply various types of tests that will cover each element of the architecture

Audience

This book is for you if you care about the architecture of the software you are building. To get the most out of this book, you must have some experience with web development. The code examples in this book are in Java. If you are not a Java programmer but can read object-oriented code in other languages, you will be fine. In the few places where Java or framework specifics are needed, they are thoroughly explained.

Approach

This book explains all concepts through an example web application called "BuckPal," which transfers money online.

The code of the example application is available on GitHub at https://github.com/thombergs/buckpal. Feel free to post any questions and suggestions as issues in the GitHub repository.

Conventions

The code examples in this book are in Java. Even as a Java fanboy, I will admit that Java is a very verbose programming language. Since I don't want you to be distracted by boilerplate code within the code examples, I decided to just leave it out. In order for the code to still be valid, I included Lombok (https://projectlombok.org) annotations in the code that will autogenerate some boilerplate code:

- The **@Getter** annotation will autogenerate getter methods for the annotated field or, if used on a class, on all private fields of that class.

- The **@RequiredArgsConstructor** annotation will autogenerate a constructor with parameters to initialize all *private final* fields of a class.

- The **@NoArgsConstructor** annotation will autogenerate a no-argument (default) constructor.

Feedback

If you have anything to say about this book, I'd love to hear it. Get in touch with me via mail at **tom@reflectoring.io** or on Twitter via https://twitter.com/TomHombergs.

What's Wrong with Layers?

Chances are that you have developed a layered (web) application in the past. You might even be doing it in your current project right now (actually, I am).

Thinking in layers has been drilled into us in computer science classes, tutorials, and best practices. It has even been taught in books (*Software Architecture Patterns by Mark Richards, O'Reilly, 2015*):

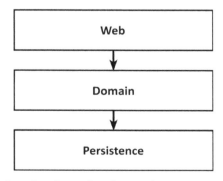

Figure 1.1: A conventional web application architecture consists of a web layer, a domain layer, and a persistence layer

The preceding figure shows a high-level view of the very common three-layer architecture. We have a **Web** layer, which receives requests and routes them to a service in the **Domain** or business layer. The service does some business magic and calls components from the **Persistence** layer to query for or modify the current state of our domain entities.

You know what? Layers are a solid architecture pattern. If we get them right, we can build domain logic that is independent of the web and persistence layers. We can switch the Web or Persistence technologies without affecting our Domain logic if we feel like it. We can add new features without affecting existing features.

With a good layered architecture, we're keeping our options open and are able to quickly adapt to changing requirements and external factors. And if we believe Uncle Bob, this is exactly what architecture is all about (*Clean Architecture by Robert C. Martin, Prentice Hall, 2017, Chapter 15*).

So, what's wrong with layers?

In my experience, a layered architecture has too many open flanks that allow bad habits to creep in and make the software increasingly hard to change over time. In the following sections, I'll tell you why.

It Promotes Database-Driven Design

By its very definition, the foundation of a conventional layered architecture is the database.

The web layer depends on the domain layer, which in turn depends on the persistence layer and thus the database.

Everything builds on top of the persistence layer. This is problematic due to several reasons.

Let's take a step back and think about what we're trying to achieve with almost any application we're building. We're typically trying to create a model of the rules or "policies" that govern the business in order to make it easier for the users to interact with them.

We're primarily trying to model behavior, and not state. Yes, state is an important part of any application, but the behavior is what changes the state and thus drives the business.

So, why are we making the *database* the foundation of our architecture and not the *domain logic*?

Think back to the last use cases you have implemented in any application. Did you start by implementing the domain logic or the persistence layer? Most likely, you thought about what the database structure would look like and only then moved on to implementing the domain logic on top of it.

This makes sense in a conventional layered architecture since we're going with the natural flow of dependencies. But it makes absolutely no sense from a business point of view. We should build the domain logic before doing anything else. Only then can we find out whether we have understood it correctly. And only once we know we're building the right domain logic should we move on to build a persistence and web layer around it.

A driving force in such a database-centric architecture is the use of object-relational mapping (ORM) frameworks. Don't get me wrong, I love those frameworks and I'm working with JPA and Hibernate on a daily basis.

But if we combine an ORM framework with a layered architecture, we're easily tempted to mix business rules with persistence aspects:

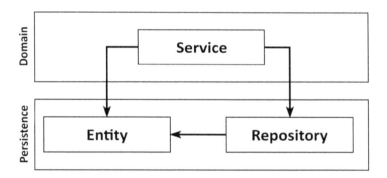

Figure 1.2: Using the database entities in the domain layer leads to strong coupling with the persistence layer

Usually, we have ORM-managed entities as part of the persistence layer, as shown in the preceding figure. Since layers may access the layers below them, the Domain layer is allowed to access those entities. And if it's allowed to use them, they *will* be used.

This creates a strong coupling between the Persistence layer and the Domain layer. Our services use the persistence model as their business model and not only have to deal with the domain logic but also with eager versus lazy loading, database transactions, flushing caches, and similar housekeeping tasks.

The persistence code is virtually fused into the domain code, and thus it's hard to change one without the other. That's the opposite of being flexible and keeping options open, which should be the goal of our architecture.

It's Prone to Shortcuts

In a conventional layered architecture, the only global rule is that from a certain layer, we can only access components in the same layer or in a layer below.

There may be other rules that a development team has agreed upon, and some of them might even be enforced by tooling, but the layered architecture style itself does not impose those rules on us.

So, if we need access to a certain component in a layer above ours, we can just push the component down a layer, and we're allowed to access it. Problem solved.

Doing this once may be OK. But doing it once opens the door for doing it a second time. And if someone else was allowed to do it, so am I, right?

I'm not saying that as developers, we take such shortcuts lightly. But if there is an option to do something, someone will do it, especially in combination with a looming deadline. And if something has been done before, the threshold for someone to do it again will lower drastically. This is a psychological effect called the "Broken Windows Theory" – more on this in *Chapter 11, Taking Shortcuts Consciously*:

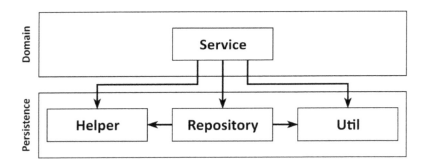

Figure 1.3: Since we may access everything in the persistence layer, it tends to grow fat over time

Over years of development and maintenance of a software project, the persistence layer may very well end up like the one in the preceding figure.

The persistence layer (or, in more generic terms, the bottom-most layer) will grow fat as we push components down through the layers. Perfect candidates for this are helper or utility components since they don't seem to belong to any specific layer.

So, if we want to disable the "shortcut mode" for our architecture, layers are not the best option, at least not without enforcing some kind of additional architecture rules. And by "enforce," I don't mean a senior developer doing code reviews but rules that make the build fail when they're broken.

It Grows Hard to Test

A common evolution within a layered architecture is that layers are being skipped. We access the Persistence layer directly from the Web layer since we're only manipulating a single field of an **Entity**, and for that we need not bother the Domain layer, right?

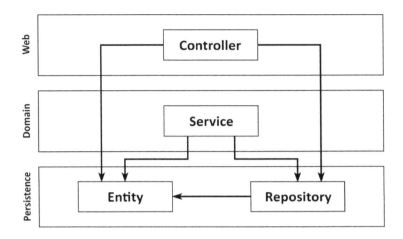

Figure 1.4: Skipping the domain layer tends to scatter domain logic across the code base

Again, this feels OK the first couple of times, but it has two drawbacks if it happens often (and it will, once someone has done the first step).

First, we're implementing domain logic in the Web layer, even if it's only manipulating a single field. What if the use case expands in the future? We're most likely going to add more domain logic to the Web layer, mixing responsibilities and spreading essential domain logic all over the application.

Second, in the tests of our Web layer, we not only have to mock away the domain layer, but also the persistence layer. This adds complexity to the unit test. And a complex test setup is the first step toward no tests at all because we don't have time for them.

As the web component grows over time, it may accumulate a lot of dependencies to different persistence components, adding to the test's complexity. At some point, it takes more time for us to understand and mock away the dependencies than to actually write test code.

It Hides the Use Cases

As developers, we like to create new code that implements shiny new use cases. But we usually spend much more time changing existing code than we do creating new code. This is not only true for those dreaded legacy projects in which we're working on a decades-old code base but also for a hot new greenfield project after the initial use cases have been implemented.

Since we're so often searching for the right place to add or change functionality, our architecture should help us to quickly navigate the code base. How is a layered architecture holding up in this regard?

As already discussed, in a layered architecture domain logic can easily be scattered throughout the layers. It may exist in the web layer if we're skipping the domain logic for an "easy" use case. And it may exist in the persistence layer if we have pushed a certain component down so it can be accessed from both the domain and the persistence layer. This already makes finding the right place to add new functionality hard.

But there's more. A layered architecture does not impose rules on the "width" of domain services. Over time, this often leads to very broad services that serve multiple use cases, as shown in the following figure:

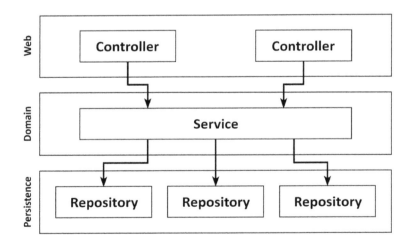

Figure 1.5: Broad services make it hard to find a certain use case within the code base

A broad service has many dependencies on the persistence layer, and many components in the web layer depend on it. This not only makes the service hard to test but also makes it hard for us to find the service that's responsible for the use case we want to work on.

How much easier would it be if we had highly specialized narrow domain services that each serve a single use case? Instead of searching for the user registration use case in the *UserService*, we would just open up the *RegisterUserService* and start working.

It Makes Parallel Work Difficult

Management usually expects us to be done with building the software they sponsor at a certain date. Actually, they even expect us to be done within a certain budget as well, but let's not complicate things here.

Aside from the fact that I have never seen "done" software in my career as a software developer, to be done by a certain date usually implies that we have to work in parallel.

Probably you know this famous conclusion from "The Mythical Man-Month," even if you haven't read the book:

> *"Adding manpower to a late software project makes it later"* – *The Mythical Man-Month: Essays on Software Engineering by Frederick P. Brooks, Jr.*, Addison-Wesley, 1995.

This also holds true, to a degree, to software projects that are not (yet) late. You cannot expect a large group of 50 developers to be 5 times as fast as a smaller team of 10 developers in every context. If they're working on a very large application where and they can split up in sub-teams and work on separate parts of the software, it may work, but in most contexts, they would stand on each other's feet.

But on a healthy scale, we can certainly expect to be faster with more people on the project. And management is right to expect that of us.

To meet this expectation, our architecture must support parallel work. This is not easy. And a layered architecture doesn't really help us here.

Imagine we're adding a new use case to our application. We have three developers available. One can add the needed features to the web layer, one to the domain layer, and the third to the persistence layer, right?

Well, it usually doesn't work that way in a layered architecture. Since everything builds on top of the persistence layer, the persistence layer must be developed first. Then comes the domain layer, and finally the web layer. So, only one developer can work on the feature at the same time.

Ah, but the developers can define interfaces first, you say, and then each developer can work against these interfaces without having to wait for the actual implementation. Sure, this is possible, but only if we're not doing database-driven design, as discussed earlier, where our persistence logic is so mixed up with our domain logic that we just cannot work on each aspect separately.

If we have broad services in our codebase, it may even be hard to work on *different* features in parallel. Working on different use cases will cause the same service to be edited in parallel, which leads to merge conflicts and, potentially, regressions.

How Does This Help Me Build Maintainable Software?

If you have built layered architectures in the past, you can probably relate to some of the disadvantages discussed in this chapter, and you could maybe even add some more.

If done correctly, and if some additional rules are imposed on it, a layered architecture can be very maintainable and make changing or adding to the codebase a breeze.

However, the discussion shows that a layered architecture allows many things to go wrong. Without very strict self-discipline, it's prone to degrade and become less maintainable over time. And this self-discipline usually becomes a little less strict each time a manager draws a new deadline around the development team.

Keeping the traps of a layered architecture in mind will help us the next time we argue against taking a shortcut and for building a more maintainable solution instead – whether in a layered architecture or a different architecture style.

Inverting Dependencies

After the rant about layered architecture in the previous chapter, you are right to expect this chapter to discuss an alternative approach. We will start by discussing the Single Responsibility Principle and the Dependency Inversion Principle. They are the "S" and the "D" of the SOLID principles, which you can read about in detail in "Clean Architecture" by Robert C. Martin or on Wikipedia at https://en.wikipedia.org/wiki/SOLID).

The Single Responsibility Principle

Everyone in software development probably knows the Single Responsibility Principle (SRP) or at least assumes they know it.

A common interpretation of this principle is this:

> A *component should do only one thing, and do it right.*

That's good advice, but not the actual intention of the SRP.

"Doing only one thing" is actually the most obvious interpretation of a single responsibility, so it's no wonder that the SRP is frequently interpreted like this. Let's just note that the name of the SRP is misleading.

Here's the actual definition of the SRP:

> *A component should have only one reason to change.*

As we can see, "responsibility" should actually be translated to "reason to change" instead of "do only one thing."

Perhaps we should rename the SRP the "Single Reason to Change Principle."

If a component has only one reason to change, it might end up doing only one thing, but the more important part is that it has only this one reason to change.

What does that mean for our architecture?

If a component has only one reason to change, we don't have to worry about this component at all if we change the software for *any other reason*, because we know that it will still work as expected.

Sadly, it's very easy for a reason to change to propagate through code via the dependencies of a component to other components; see the following figure:

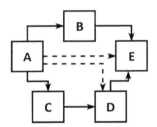

Figure 2.1: Each dependency of a component is a possible reason to change this component, even if it is only a transitive dependency (dashed arrows)

In the preceding figure, component A depends on many other components (either directly or transitively) while component E has no dependencies at all.

The only reason to change component E is when the functionality of E must change due to a new requirement. Component A, however, might have to change when any of the other components change because it depends on them.

Many codebases grow harder – and thus more expensive – to change over time because the SRP is violated. Over time, components collect more and more reasons to change. After having collected many reasons to change, changing one component might cause another component to fail.

A Tale about Side Effects

I once was part of a project where my team inherited a 10-year-old code base built by another software shop. The client had decided to replace the development team to make maintenance and development better and less expensive in the future.

As was to be expected, it was not easy to gain an understanding of what the code actually did, and changes we made in one area of the codebase often had side effects in other areas. But we managed – by testing exhaustively, adding automated tests, and refactoring a lot.

After some time of successfully maintaining and extending the code base, the client requested a new feature to be implemented in a way that struck me as very awkward for the users of the software. So, I proposed to do it in a more user-friendly way that was even less expensive to implement since it needed fewer overall changes. It needed a small change in a certain very central component, however.

The client declined and ordered the more awkward and expensive solution. When I asked the reason for this, they said that they were afraid of side effects because changes in that one component by the previous development team had always broken something else in the past.

Sadly, this is an example of how you can train your client to pay extra for modifying badly architected software. Luckily, most clients will not play along with this game, so let's try to build good software instead.

The Dependency Inversion Principle

In our layered architecture, the cross-layer dependencies always point downward, to the next layer. When we apply the SRP on a high level, we notice that the upper layers have more reasons to change than the lower layers.

Thus, due to the domain layer's dependency on the persistence layer, each change in the persistence layer potentially requires a change in the domain layer. But the domain code is the most important code in our application. We don't want to have to change it when something changes in the persistence code.

So, how can we get rid of this dependency?

The Dependency Inversion Principle (DIP) provides the answer.

In contrast to the SRP, the DIP means what the name suggests:

> *We can turn around (invert) the direction of any dependency within our codebase.*

Actually, we can only invert dependencies when we have control over the code on both sides of the dependency. If we have a dependency on a third-party library, we cannot invert it, since we don't control the code of that library.

How does that work? Let's try to invert the dependency between our domain and persistence code so that the persistence code depends on the domain code, reducing the number of reasons to change the domain code.

We start with a structure such as the one in *Figure 1.2* from *Chapter 1, What's Wrong with Layers?* We have a service in the domain layer that works with entities and repositories from the persistence layer.

First of all, we want to pull up the entities into the domain layer because they represent our domain objects and our domain code pretty much revolves around changing state in those entities.

But now, we will have a circular dependency between both layers since the repository from the persistence layer depends on the entity, which is now in the domain layer. This is where we apply the DIP. We create an interface for the repository in the domain layer and let the actual repository in the persistence layer implement it. The result is something like what you see in the following figure:

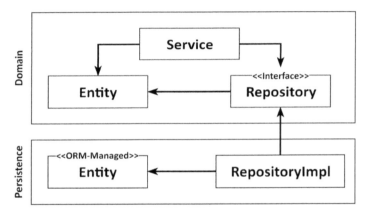

Figure 2.2: By introducing an interface in the domain layer, we can invert the dependency so that the persistence layer depends on the domain layer

With this trick, we have liberated our domain logic from the oppressive dependency on the persistence code. This is a core feature of the two architecture styles we are going to discuss in the upcoming sections.

Clean Architecture

Robert C. Martin cemented the term "clean architecture" in his book of the same name (*Clean Architecture by Robert C. Martin, Prentice Hall, 2017, Chapter 22*). In clean architecture, in his opinion, the business rules are testable by design and independent of frameworks, databases, UI technologies, and other external applications or interfaces.

That means that the domain code must not have any outward-facing dependencies. Instead, with the help of the DIP, all dependencies point toward the domain code.

The following figure shows how such an architecture might look on an abstract level:

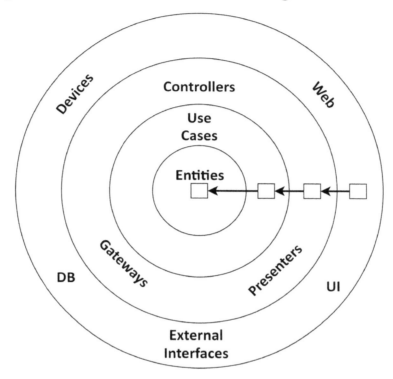

Figure 2.3: In a clean architecture, all dependencies point inward toward the domain logic.
Source: "Clean Architecture" by Robert C. Martin

The layers in this architecture are wrapped around each other in concentric circles. The main rule in such an architecture is the dependency rule, which states that all dependencies between those layers must point inward.

The core of the architecture contains the domain entities, which are accessed by the surrounding use cases. The use cases are what we have called services earlier but are more fine-grained to have a single responsibility (that is, a single reason to change), thus avoiding the problem of *broad services* that we discussed earlier.

Around this core, we can find all the other components of our application that support the business rules. This support can mean providing persistence or providing a UI, for example. Also, the outer layers may provide adapters to any other third-party component.

Since the domain code knows nothing about which persistence or UI framework is used, it cannot contain any code specific to those frameworks and will concentrate on the business rules. We have all the freedom we could wish for to model the domain code. We could, for example, apply Domain-Driven Design (DDD) in its purest form. Not having to think about persistence or UI-specific problems makes that so much easier.

As we might expect, clean architecture comes at a cost. Since the domain layer is completely decoupled from the outer layers, such as persistence and UI, we have to maintain a model of our application's entities in each of the layers.

Let's assume, for instance, that we are using an **object-relational mapping (ORM)** framework in our persistence layer. An ORM framework usually expects specific entity classes that contain metadata describing the database structure and the mapping of object fields to database columns. Since the domain layer doesn't know the persistence layer, we cannot use the same entity classes in the domain layer and have to create them in both layers. That means we have to translate between both representations when the domain layer sends and receives data to and from the persistence layer. The same translation applies between the domain layer and other outer layers.

But that's a good thing. This decoupling is exactly what we wanted to achieve to free the domain code from framework-specific problems. The Java Persistence API (the standard ORM-API in the Java world), for instance, requires ORM-managed entities to have a default constructor without arguments that we might want to avoid in our domain model. In *Chapter 8, Mapping between Boundaries*, we will talk about different mapping strategies, including a "no-mapping" strategy that just accepts the coupling between the domain and persistence layers.

Since the clean architecture by Robert C. Martin is somewhat abstract, let's go a level of detail deeper and look at a "hexagonal architecture," which gives the clean architecture principles a more concrete shape.

Hexagonal Architecture

The term "hexagonal architecture" stems from Alistair Cockburn and has been around for quite some time (The primary source for the term "Hexagonal Architecture" is Alistair Cockburn's blog post at https://alistair.cockburn.us/hexagonal-architecture/). It applies the same principles that Robert C. Martin later described in more general terms in his *clean architecture*:

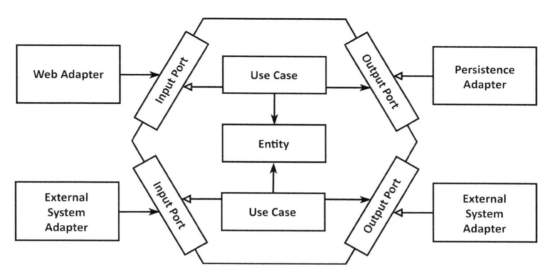

Figure 2.4: A hexagonal architecture is also called a "ports-and-adapters" architecture since the application core provides specific ports for each adapter to interact with

The preceding figure shows what a hexagonal architecture might look like. The application core is represented as a hexagon, giving this architecture style its name. The hexagon shape has no meaning, however, so we might just as well draw an octagon and call it "octagonal architecture." According to legend, the hexagon was simply used instead of the common rectangle to show that an application can have more than four sides connecting it to other systems or adapters.

Within the hexagon, we find our domain entities and the use cases that work with them. Note that the hexagon has no outgoing dependencies, so the dependency rule from Martin's clean architecture holds true. Instead, all dependencies point toward the center.

Outside of the hexagon, we find various adapters that interact with the application. There might be a web adapter that interacts with a web browser, some adapters interacting with external systems, and an adapter that interacts with a database.

The adapters on the left-hand side are adapters that drive our application (because they call our application core) while the adapters on the right-hand side are driven by our application (because they are called by our application core).

To allow communication between the application core and the adapters, the application core provides specific ports. For driving adapters, such a port might be an interface that is implemented by one of the use case classes in the core and called by the adapter. For a driven adapter, it might be an interface that is implemented by the adapter and called by the core.

Due to its central concepts, this architecture style is also known as a "ports-and-adapters" architecture. Just like clean architecture, we can organize this hexagonal architecture into layers. The outermost layer consists of the adapters that translate between the application and other systems. Next, we can combine the ports and use case implementations to form the application layer, because they define the interface of our application. The final layer contains the domain entities.

In the next chapter, we will discuss a way to organize such an architecture in code.

How Does This Help Me Build Maintainable Software?

Call it clean architecture, hexagonal architecture, or ports-and-adapters architecture – by inverting our dependencies so that the domain code has no dependencies to the outside, we can decouple our domain logic from all those persistence and UI-specific problems and reduce the number of reasons to make changes throughout the codebase. And fewer reasons to change means better maintainability.

The domain code is free to be modeled as best fits the business problems while the persistence and UI code is free to be modeled as best fits the persistence and UI problems.

In the rest of this book, we will apply the hexagonal architecture style to a web application. We'll start by creating the package structure of our application and discussing the role of dependency injection.

3

Organizing Code

Wouldn't it be nice to recognize an architecture just by looking at the code?

In this chapter, we will examine different ways of organizing code and introduce an expressive package structure that directly reflects a hexagonal architecture.

In greenfield software projects, the first thing we try to get right is the package structure. We set up a nice-looking structure that we intend to use for the rest of the project. Then, during the project, things become hectic and we realize that in many places the package structure is just a nice-looking facade for an unstructured mess of code. Classes in one package import classes from other packages that should not be imported.

We will discuss different options for structuring the code of the BuckPal example application that was introduced in the preface. More specifically, we will look at the "Send Money" use case, with which a user can transfer money from their account to another.

Organizing by Layer

The first approach to organizing our code is by layer. We might organize a code like this:

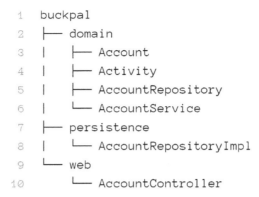

```
1   buckpal
2   ├── domain
3   │    ├── Account
4   │    ├── Activity
5   │    ├── AccountRepository
6   │    └── AccountService
7   ├── persistence
8   │    └── AccountRepositoryImpl
9   └── web
10       └── AccountController
```

Figure 3.1: When organizing code by layer, functional aspects tend to be mixed

For each of our layers, **web**, **domain**, and **persistence**, we have a dedicated package. As discussed in *Chapter 1, What's Wrong with Layers?*, simple layers may not be the best structure for our code for several reasons, so we have already applied the Dependency Inversion Principle here, only allowing dependencies toward the domain code in the **domain** package. We did this by introducing the **AccountRepository** interface in the **domain** package and implementing it in the **persistence** package.

However, we can find at least three reasons why this package structure is suboptimal.

First, we have no package boundary between functional slices or features of our application. If we add a feature for managing users, we will add a **UserController** to the **web** package, a **UserService**, **UserRepository**, and **User** to the **domain** package and a **UserRepositoryImpl** to the **persistence** package. Without further structure, this might quickly become a mess of classes, leading to unwanted side effects between supposedly unrelated features of the application.

Second, we can't see what use cases our application provides. Can you tell what use cases the **AccountService** or **AccountController** classes implement? If we are looking for a certain feature, we have to guess what service implements it and then search for the responsible method within that service.

Similarly, we can't see our target architecture within the package structure. We can guess that we have followed the hexagonal architecture style and then browse the classes in the **web** and **persistence** packages to find the web and persistence adapters. But we can't see at a glance what functionality is called by the web adapter and what functionality the persistence adapter provides for the domain layer. The incoming and outgoing ports are hidden in the code.

Organizing by Feature

Let's try to address some of the issues of the "organize by layer" approach.

The next approach is to organize our code by feature:

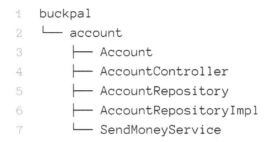

```
1  buckpal
2  └── account
3       ├── Account
4       ├── AccountController
5       ├── AccountRepository
6       ├── AccountRepositoryImpl
7       └── SendMoneyService
```

Figure 3.2: When organizing code by feature, the underlying architecture tends not to be apparent

In essence, we have put all the code related to accounts into the high-level **account** package. We have also removed the layer packages.

Each new group of features will get a new high-level package next to **account** and we can enforce package boundaries between the features by using package-private visibility for the classes that should not be accessed from the outside.

The package boundaries, combined with package-private visibility, enable us to avoid unwanted dependencies between features.

We have also renamed **AccountService** to **SendMoneyService** to narrow its responsibility (we actually could have done that in the package-by-layer approach, too). We can now see that the code implements the "Send Money" use case just by looking at the class names. Making the application's functionality visible in the code is what Robert Martin calls a "screaming architecture," because it screams its intention at us (*Clean Architecture by Robert C. Martin, Prentice Hall, 2017, Chapter 21*).

However, the package-by-feature approach makes our architecture *even less visible* than the package-by-layer approach. We have no package names to identify our adapters, and we still don't see the incoming and outgoing ports. What's more, even though we have inverted the dependencies between the domain code and the persistence code so that **SendMoneyService** only knows the **AccountRepository** interface and not its implementation, we cannot use package-private visibility to protect the domain code from accidental dependencies to persistence code.

So, how can we make our target architecture visible at a glance? It would be nice if we could point a finger at a box in an architecture diagram such as the one shown in *Figure 2.4* and instantly know what part of the code is responsible for that box.

Let's take one more step to create a package structure that is expressive enough to support this.

An Architecturally Expressive Package Structure

In a hexagonal architecture, we have entities, use cases, incoming and outgoing ports, and incoming and outgoing (or "driving" and "driven") adapters as our main architectural elements. Let's fit them into a package structure that expresses this architecture:

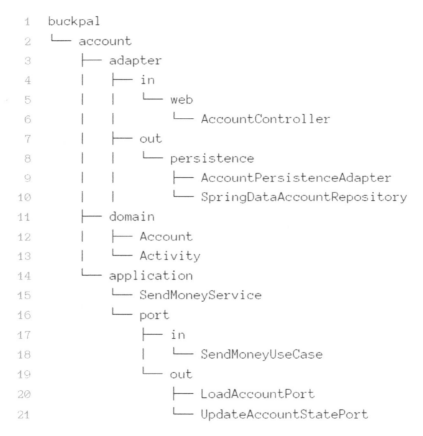

Figure 3.3: In an architecturally expressive package structure, each architecture element has its place

Each element of the architecture can directly be mapped to one of the packages. At the highest level, we again have a package named **account**, indicating that this is the module implementing the use cases around an **Account**.

On the next level, we have the **domain** package containing our domain model. The **application** package contains a service layer around this domain model. **SendMoneyService** implements the incoming port interface, **SendMoneyUseCase**, and uses the outgoing port interfaces, **LoadAccountPort** and **UpdateAccountStatePort**, which are implemented by the persistence adapter.

The **adapter** package contains the incoming adapters that call the application layers' incoming ports and the outgoing adapters that provide implementations for the application layers' outgoing ports. In our case, we are building a simple web application with the **web** and **persistence** adapters, each having its own sub-package.

Phew, that's a lot of technical-sounding packages. Isn't that confusing?

Imagine we have a high-level view of our hexagonal architecture hanging on the office wall and we are talking to a colleague about modifying a client to a third-party API we are consuming. While discussing this, we can point at the corresponding outgoing adapter on the poster to better understand each other. Then, when we are finished talking, we sit down in front of our IDE and can start working on the client right away, because the code of the API client we have talked about can be found in the *adapter/ out/<name-of-adapter>* package.

Rather helpful instead of confusing, don't you think?

This package structure is a powerful element in the fight against the so-called "architecture-code gap" or "model-code gap" (*Just Enough Architecture by George Fairbanks, Marshall & Brainerd, 2010, page 167*). These terms describe the fact that in most software development projects the architecture is only an abstract concept that cannot be directly mapped to the code. With time, if the package structure (among other things) does not reflect the architecture, the code will usually deviate more and more from the target architecture.

Also, this expressive package structure promotes active thinking about architecture. We have many packages and have to think about into which package to put the code we are currently working on.

But doesn't having so many packages mean that everything has to be public in order to allow access across packages?

For the adapter packages, at least, this is not true. All classes they contain may be package-private since they are not called by the outside world except over port interfaces that live within the **application** package. So, no accidental dependencies from the application layer to the adapter classes.

Within the **application** and **domain** packages, however, some classes indeed have to be public. The ports must be public because they must be accessible to the adapters by design. The domain classes must be public to be accessible by the services and, potentially, by the adapters. The services don't need to be public, because they can be hidden behind the incoming port interfaces.

Moving the adapter code to its own packages has the added benefit that we can very easily replace one adapter with another implementation, should the need arise. Imagine we have started implementing against a simple key-value database, because we weren't sure about what database would be best in the end, and now we need to switch to a SQL database. We simply implement all relevant outgoing ports in a new adapter package and then remove the old package.

Another very appealing advantage of this package structure is that it directly maps to DDD concepts. The high-level package, **account**, in our case, is a bounded context that has dedicated entry and exit points (the ports) to communicate with other bounded contexts. Within the **domain** package, we can build any domain model we want, using all the tools DDD provides us.

As with every structure, it takes discipline to maintain this package structure over the lifetime of a software project. Also, there will be cases when the package structure just does not fit, and we see no other way than to widen the architecture/code gap and create a package that does not reflect the architecture.

There is no such thing as perfection. But with an expressive package structure, we can at least reduce the gap between code and architecture.

The Role of Dependency Injection

The package structure described previously goes a long way toward a clean architecture, but an essential requirement of such an architecture is that the application layer does not have dependencies on the incoming and outgoing adapters, as we learned in *Chapter 2, Inverting Dependencies*.

For incoming adapters, such as our web adapter, this is easy, since the control flow points in the same direction as the dependency between the adapter and domain code. The adapter simply calls the service within the application layer. In order to clearly demarcate the entry points to our application, we might want to hide the actual services between port interfaces, nonetheless.

For outgoing adapters, such as our persistence adapter, we have to make use of the Dependency Inversion Principle to turn the dependency against the direction of the control flow.

We have already seen how that works. We create an interface within the application layer that is implemented by a class within the adapter. Within our hexagonal architecture, this interface is a port. The application layer then calls this port interface to call the functionality of the adapter as shown in the following figure:

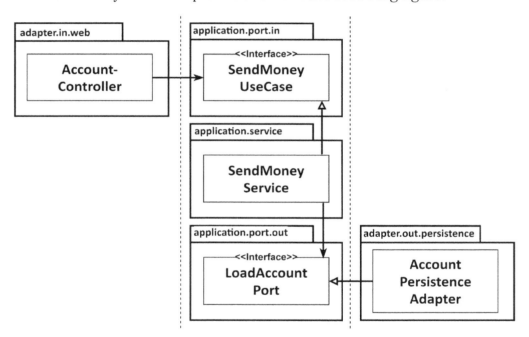

Figure 3.4: The web controller calls an incoming port, which is implemented by a service. The service calls an outgoing port, which is implemented by an adapter

But who provides the application with the actual objects that implement the port interfaces? We don't want to instantiate the ports manually within the application layer, because we don't want to introduce a dependency to an adapter.

This is where dependency injection comes into play. We introduce a neutral component that has a dependency on all layers. This component is responsible for instantiating most of the classes that make up our architecture.

In the preceding example figure, the neutral dependency injection component would create instances of the **AccountController**, **SendMoneyService**, and **AccountPersistenceAdapter** classes. Since **AccountController** requires a **SendMoneyUseCase** interface, the dependency injection will give it an instance of the **SendMoneyService** class during construction. The controller doesn't know that it actually has a **SendMoneyService** instance since it only needs to know the interface.

Similarly, when constructing the **SendMoneyService** instance, the dependency injection mechanism will inject an instance of the **AccountPersistenceAdapter** class, in the guise of the **LoadAccountPort** interface. The service never knows the actual class behind the interface.

We will talk more about initializing an application using the Spring Framework as an example in *Chapter 9, Assembling the Application*.

How Does This Help Me Build Maintainable Software?

We have looked at a package structure for hexagonal architecture that takes the actual code structure as close to the target architecture as possible. Finding an element of the architecture in the code is now a matter of navigating down the package structure along with the names of certain boxes in an architecture diagram, helping in communication, development, and maintenance.

In the following chapters, we will see this package structure and dependency injection in action as we are going to implement a use case in the application layer, a web adapter, and a persistence adapter.

Implementing a
Use Case

Let's finally look at how we can manifest the architecture we have discussed in actual code.

Since the application, web, and persistence layers are so loosely coupled in our architecture, we are totally free to model our domain code as we see fit. We can do DDD, we can implement a rich or an anemic domain model, or we can invent our own way of doing things.

This chapter describes an opinionated way of implementing use cases within the hexagonal architecture style that we have introduced in the previous chapters.

As is fitting for a domain-centric architecture, we will start with a domain entity and then build a use case around it.

Implementing the Domain Model

We want to implement the use case of sending money from one account to another. One way to model this in object-oriented fashion is to create an **Account** entity that allows us to withdraw and deposit money so that we can withdraw money from the source account and deposit it into the target account:

```
package buckpal.domain;


public class Account {

  private AccountId id;
  private Money baselineBalance;
  private ActivityWindow activityWindow;


  // constructors and getters omitted


  public Money calculateBalance() {
    return Money.add(
          this.baselineBalance,
          this.activityWindow.calculateBalance(this.id));
  }


  public boolean withdraw(Money, AccountId targetAccountId) {

    if (!mayWithdraw(money)) {
      return false;
    }

    Activity withdrawal = new Activity(
        this.id,
        this.id,
        targetAccountId,
```

```
            LocalDateTime.now(),
            money);
      this.activityWindow.addActivity(withdrawal);
      return true;
   }


   private boolean mayWithdraw(Money money) {
      return Money.add(
            this.calculateBalance(),
            money.negate())
            .isPositive();
   }


   public boolean deposit(Money, AccountId sourceAccountId) {
      Activity deposit = new Activity(
            this.id,
            sourceAccountId,
            this.id,
            LocalDateTime.now(),
            money);
      this.activityWindow.addActivity(deposit);
      return true;
   }


}
```

The **Account** entity provides the current snapshot of an actual account. Every withdrawal from and deposit into an account is captured in an **Activity** entity. Since it would not be wise to always load *all* activities of an account into memory, the **Account** entity only holds a window of the last few days or weeks of activities, captured in the **ActivityWindow** value object.

To still be able to calculate the current account balance, the `Account` entity additionally has the `baselineBalance` attribute, representing the balance the account had just before the first activity of the activity window. The total balance then is the baseline balance plus the balance of all activities in the window.

With this model, withdrawing and depositing money from and into an account is a matter of adding a new activity to the activity window, as is done in the `withdraw()` and `deposit()` methods. Before we can withdraw, we check the business rule that says that we cannot overdraw an account.

Now that we have an `Account` entity that allows us to withdraw and deposit money, we can move outward to build a use case around it.

A Use Case in a Nutshell

First, let's discuss what a use case actually does. Usually, it follows these steps:

1. Takes input

2. Validates business rules

3. Manipulates the model state

4. Returns output

A use case takes input from an incoming adapter. You might wonder why I didn't call this step "Validate input." The answer is that I believe use case code should care about the domain logic and we shouldn't pollute it with input validation. So, we will do input validation somewhere else, as we will see shortly.

The use case is, however, responsible for validating *business rules*. It shares this responsibility with the domain entities. We will discuss the distinction between input validation and business rule validation later in this chapter.

If the business rules were satisfied, the use case then manipulates the state of the model in one way or another, based on the input. Usually, it will change the state of a domain object and pass this new state to a port implemented by the persistence adapter to be persisted. A use case might also call any other outgoing adapters, though.

The last step is to translate the return value from the outgoing adapter into an output object, which will be returned to the calling adapter.

With these steps in mind, let's see how we can implement our "Send Money" use case.

To avoid the problem of broad services discussed in *Chapter 1, What's Wrong with Layers?*, we will create a separate service class for each use case instead of putting all use cases into a single service class.

Here's a teaser:

```java
package buckpal.application.service;


@RequiredArgsConstructor
@Transactional
public class SendMoneyService implements SendMoneyUseCase {

  private final LoadAccountPort loadAccountPort;
  private final AccountLock accountLock;
  private final UpdateAccountStatePort updateAccountStatePort;


  @Override
  public boolean sendMoney(SendMoneyCommand command) {
    // TODO: validate business rules
    // TODO: manipulate model state
    // TODO: return output
  }
}
```

The service implements the incoming port interface, **SendMoneyUseCase**, and will call the outgoing port interface, **LoadAccountPort**, to load an account, and calls **UpdateAccountStatePort** to persist an updated account state in the database. The following figure gives a graphical overview of the relevant components:

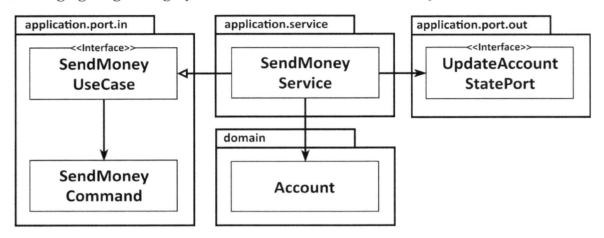

Figure 4.1: A service implements a use case, modifies the domain model,
and calls an outgoing port to persist the modified state

Let's take care of those **// TODO**s we left in the preceding code.

Validating Input

Now we are talking about validating input, even though I just claimed that it's not a responsibility of a use case class. I still think, however, that it belongs to the application layer, so this is the place to discuss it.

Why not let the calling adapter validate the input before sending it to the use case? Well, do we want to trust the caller to have validated everything as is needed for the use case? Also, the use case might be called by more than one adapter, so the validation would have to be implemented by each adapter and we might get it wrong or forget it altogether.

The application layer should care about input validation because, well, otherwise it might get invalid input from outside the application core, and this might cause damage to the state of our model.

But where to put the input validation if not in the use case class?

We will let the *input model* take care of it. For the "Send Money" use case, the input model is the **SendMoneyCommand** class we have already seen in the previous code example. More precisely, we will do it within the constructor:

```
package buckpal.application.port.in;


@Getter
public class SendMoneyCommand {


    private final AccountId sourceAccountId;
    private final AccountId targetAccountId;
    private final Money;


    public SendMoneyCommand(
            AccountId sourceAccountId,
            AccountId targetAccountId,
            Money money) {
        this.sourceAccountId = sourceAccountId;
        this.targetAccountId = targetAccountId;
        this.money = money;
        requireNonNull(sourceAccountId);
        requireNonNull(targetAccountId);
        requireNonNull(money);
        requireGreaterThan(money, 0);
    }
}
```

For sending money, we need the IDs of the source and target account and the amount of money that is to be transferred. None of the parameters must be null and the amount must be greater than zero. If any of these conditions is violated, we simply refuse object creation by throwing an exception during construction.

By making the fields of **SendMoneyCommand** final, we effectively make it immutable. So, once constructed successfully, we can be sure that the state is valid and cannot be changed to something invalid.

Since **SendMoneyCommand** is part of the use case API, it's located in the incoming port package. Thus, the validation remains in the core of the application (within the hexagon of our hexagonal architecture) but does not pollute the sacred use case code.

But do we really want to implement each validation check by hand when there are tools that can do the dirty work for us? In the Java world, the de facto standard for this kind of work is the Bean Validation API (https://beanvalidation.org/). It allows us to express the validation rules we need as annotations on the fields of a class:

```
package buckpal.application.port.in;


@Getter
public class SendMoneyCommand extends SelfValidating<SendMoneyCommand> {


  @NotNull
  private final Account.AccountId sourceAccountId;
  @NotNull
  private final Account.AccountId targetAccountId;
  @NotNull
  private final Money;


  public SendMoneyCommand(
          Account.AccountId sourceAccountId,
          Account.AccountId targetAccountId,
          Money money) {
    this.sourceAccountId = sourceAccountId;
    this.targetAccountId = targetAccountId;
    this.money = money;
    requireGreaterThan(money, 0);
    this.validateSelf();
  }
}
```

The **SelfValidating** abstract class provides the **validateSelf()** method, which we simply call as the last statement in the constructor. This will evaluate the Bean Validation annotations on the fields (**@NotNull**, in this case) and throw an exception in the case of a violation. If Bean Validation is not expressive enough for a certain validation, we can still implement it by hand, as we did to check that the amount is greater than zero.

The implementation of the **SelfValidating** class might look like this:

```
package shared;


public abstract class SelfValidating<T> {


  private Validator;


  public SelfValidating(){
    ValidatorFactory factory = Validation.buildDefaultValidatorFactory();
    validator = factory.getValidator();
  }


  protected void validateSelf() {
    Set<ConstraintViolation<T>> violations = validator.validate((T) this);
    if (!violations.isEmpty()) {
      throw new ConstraintViolationException(violations);
    }
  }


}
```

With validation located in the input model, we have effectively created an anti-corruption layer around our use case implementations. This is not a layer in the sense of a layered architecture, calling the next layer below, but is instead a thin, protective screen around our use cases that bounces bad input back to the caller.

The Power of Constructors

The preceding input model, **SendMoneyCommand**, puts a lot of responsibility on its constructor. Since the class is immutable, the constructor's argument list contains a parameter for each attribute of the class. And since the constructor also validates the parameters, it's not possible to create an object with an invalid state.

In our case, the constructor has only three parameters. What if we had more parameters? Couldn't we use the **Builder** pattern to make it more convenient to use? We could make the constructor with the long parameter list private and hide the call to it in the **build()** method of our builder. Then, instead of having to call a constructor with 20 parameters, we could build an object like this:

```
new SendMoneyCommandBuilder()

    .sourceAccountId(new AccountId(41L))

    .targetAccountId(new AccountId(42L))

    // ... initialize many other fields

    .build();
```

We could still let our constructor do the validation so that the builder cannot construct an object with invalid state.

Sounds good? Think about what happens if we have to add another field to **SendMoneyCommandBuilder** (which will happen quite a few times in the lifetime of a software project). We add the new field to the constructor and to the builder. Then, a colleague (or a phone call, an email, or a butterfly...) interrupts our train of thought. After the break, we go back to coding and *forget to add the new field to the code that calls the builder*.

We don't get a word of warning from the compiler about trying to create an immutable object in an invalid state. Sure, at runtime – hopefully in a unit test – our validation logic will still kick in and throw an error because we missed a parameter.

But if we use the constructor directly instead of hiding it behind a builder, each time a new field is added or an existing field is removed, we can just follow the trail of compile errors to reflect that change in the rest of the codebase.

Long parameter lists can even be formatted nicely, and good IDEs help with parameter name hints:

```
new ClassWithManyFields(
        name: "Donald",
        LocalDate.of( year: 1934, month: 6, dayOfMonth: 9),
        socialSecurityNumber: "1234567",
        birthplace: "Duckburg",
        street: "Duckstreet 42",
        city: "Duckburg",
        zipcode: "12345",
        country: "USA",
        state: "Calisota");
```

Figure 4.2: The IDE shows parameter name hints in parameter lists to help us to not get lost

So, why not let the compiler guide us?

Different Input Models for Different Use Cases

We might be tempted to use the same input model for different use cases. Let's consider the use cases "Register Account" and "Update Account Details." Both will initially need almost the same input, namely some account details such as a description of the account.

The difference is that the "Update Account Details" use case also needs the ID of the account to be able to update that specific account. And the "Register Account" use case might need the ID of the owner, so that it can assign it to him or her. So, if we share the same input model between both use cases, we'd have to allow a **null** account ID to be passed into the "Update Account Details" use case and a **null** owner ID to be passed into the "Register Account" use case.

Allowing **null** as a valid state of a field in our immutable command object is a code smell by itself. But more importantly, how are we handling input validation now? Validation has to be different for the register and update use cases since each needs an ID the other doesn't. We'd have to build custom validation logic into the use cases themselves, polluting our sacred business code with input validation concerns.

Also, what do we do if the account ID field accidentally has a non-null value in the "Register Account" use case? Do we throw an error? Do we simply ignore it? These are the questions maintenance engineers – including future us – will ask when seeing the code.

A dedicated input model for each use case makes the use case much clearer and also decouples it from other use cases, preventing unwanted side effects. It comes with a cost, however, because we have to map incoming data into different input models for different use cases. We will discuss this mapping strategy along with other mapping strategies in *Chapter 8, Mapping between Boundaries*.

Validating Business Rules

While validating input is not part of the use case logic, validating business rules definitely is. Business rules are the core of the application and should be handled with appropriate care. But when are we dealing with input validation and when are we dealing with business rule validation?

A very pragmatic distinction between the two is that validating a business rule requires access to the current state of the domain model while validating input does not. Input validation can be implemented declaratively, as we did with the `@NotNull` annotations, while a business rule needs more context.

We might also say that input validation is a *syntactical* validation, while a business rule is a *semantical* validation in the context of a use case.

Let's take the rule "the source account must not be overdrawn." By the definition above, this is a business rule since it needs access to the current state of the model to check whether the source and target accounts do exist.

In contrast, the rule "the transfer amount must be greater than zero" can be validated without access to the model and thus can be implemented as part of the input validation.

I'm aware that this distinction may be subject to debate. You might argue that the transfer amount is so important that validating it should be considered a business rule in any case.

The distinction above helps us, however, to place certain validations within the code base and easily find them again later on. It's as simple as answering the question of whether the validation needs access to the current model state or not. This not only helps us to implement the rule in the first place, but it also helps the future maintenance engineer to find it again.

So, how do we implement a business rule?

The best way is to do put the business rules into a domain entity as we did for the rule "the source account must not be overdrawn":

```
package buckpal.domain;


public class Account {


  // ...


  public boolean withdraw(Money, AccountId targetAccountId) {
    if (!mayWithdraw(money)) {
      return false;
    }
    // ...
  }

}
```

This way, the business rule is easy to locate and reason about, because it's right next to the business logic that requires this rule to be honored.

If it's not feasible to validate a business rule in a domain entity, we can simply do it in the use case code before it starts working on the domain entities:

```
package buckpal.application.service;


@RequiredArgsConstructor

@Transactional

public class SendMoneyService implements SendMoneyUseCase {


  // ...
```

```
@Override
public boolean sendMoney(SendMoneyCommand command) {
    requireAccountExists(command.getSourceAccountId());
    requireAccountExists(command.getTargetAccountId());
    ...
  }
}
```

We simply call a method that does the actual validation and throws a dedicated exception in the case that this validation fails. The adapter interfacing with the user can then display this exception to the user as an error message or handle it any other way that seems fit.

In the preceding case, the validation simply checks if the source and target accounts actually exist in the database. More complex business rules might require us to load the domain model from the database first and then do some checks on its state. If we have to load the domain model anyway, we should implement the business rule in the domain entities themselves, as we did with the rule "the source account must not be overdrawn" previously.

Rich versus Anemic Domain Model

Our architecture style leaves open how to implement our domain model. This is a blessing because we can do what seems right in our context, and a curse because we don't have any guidelines to help us.

A frequent discussion is whether to implement a rich domain model following the DDD philosophy or an "anemic" domain model. I'm not going to favor one of the two, but let's discuss how each of them fits into our architecture.

In a rich domain model, as much of the domain logic as possible is implemented within the entities at the core of the application. The entities provide methods to change state and only allow changes that are valid according to the business rules. This is the way we pursued with the **Account** entity previously.

Where is our use case implementation in this scenario?

In this case, our use case serves as an entry point to the domain model. A use case then only represents the intent of the user and translates it into orchestrated method calls to the domain entities, which do the actual work. Many of the business rules are located in the entities instead of the use case implementation.

The "Send Money" use case service would load the source and target account entities, call their `withdraw()` and `deposit()` methods, and send them back to the database. Actually, the use case would also have to make sure that no other money transfer to and from the source and target account is happening at the same time, to avoid overdrawing an account, but we'll skip this business rule for the sake of simplicity.

In an "anemic" domain model, the entities themselves are very thin. They usually only provide fields to hold the state and getter and setter methods to read and change it. They don't contain any domain logic.

This means that the domain logic is implemented in use case classes. They are responsible for validating business rules, changing the state of the entities, and passing them into the outgoing ports responsible for storing them in the database. The "richness" is contained within the use cases instead of the entities.

Both styles and any number of other styles can be implemented using the architecture approach discussed in this book. Feel free to choose the one that fits your needs.

Different Output Models for Different Use Cases

Once the use case has done its work, what should it return to the caller?

Similar to the input, it has benefits if the output is as specific to the use case as possible. The output should only include the data that is really needed for the caller to work.

In the preceding example code of the "Send Money" use case, we returned a `boolean`. This is the minimal and most specific value we could possibly return in this context.

We might be tempted to return a complete `Account` with the updated entity to the caller. Perhaps the caller is interested in the new balance of the account.

But do we really want to make the "Send Money" use case return this data? Does the caller really need it? If so, shouldn't we create a dedicated use case for accessing that data that can be used by different callers?

There is no right answer to these questions. But we should ask them to try to keep our use cases as specific as possible. When in doubt, return as little as possible.

Sharing the same output model between use cases also tends to tightly couple those use cases. If one of the use cases needs a new field in the output model, the other use cases have to handle this field as well, even if it's irrelevant for them. Shared models tend to grow for multiple reasons in the long run. Applying the single responsibility principle and keeping models separated helps to decouple use cases.

For the same reason, we might want to resist the temptation to use our domain entities as output models. We don't want our domain entities to change for more reasons than necessary. However, we will talk more about using entities as input or output models in *Chapter 11, Taking Shortcuts Consciously.*

What about Read-Only Use Cases?

Previously, we have discussed how we might implement a use case that modifies the state of our model. How do we go about implementing read-only cases?

Let's assume the UI needs to display the balance of an account. Do we create a specific use case implementation for this?

It's awkward to talk of use cases for read-only operations like this one. Sure, in the UI, the requested data is needed to implement a certain use case we might call "View Account Balance." If this is considered a use case in the context of the project, by all means we should implement it just like the other ones.

From the viewpoint of the application core, however, this is a simple query for data. So, if it's not considered a use case in the context of the project, we can implement it as a query to set it apart from the real use cases.

One way of doing this within our architecture style is to create a dedicated incoming port for the query and implement it in a "query service":

```
package buckpal.application.service;


@RequiredArgsConstructor

class GetAccountBalanceService implements GetAccountBalanceQuery {


  private final LoadAccountPort loadAccountPort;


  @Override

  public Money getAccountBalance(AccountId accountId) {
    return loadAccountPort.loadAccount(accountId, LocalDateTime.now())
        .calculateBalance();
  }

}
```

The query service acts just as our use case services do. It implements an incoming port we named **GetAccountBalanceQuery** and calls the outgoing port, **LoadAccountPort**, to actually load the data from the database.

This way, read-only queries are clearly distinguishable from modifying use cases (or "commands") in our codebase. This plays nicely with concepts such as Command-Query Separation (CQS) and Command-Query Responsibility Segregation (CQRS).

In the preceding code, the service doesn't really do any work other than passing the query on to the outgoing port. If we use the same model across layers, we can take a shortcut and let the client call the outgoing port directly. We will talk about this shortcut in *Chapter 11, Taking Shortcuts Consciously*.

How Does This Help Me Build Maintainable Software?

Our architecture lets us implement the domain logic as we see fit, but if we model the input and output of our use cases independently, we avoid unwanted side effects.

Yes, it's more work than just sharing models between use cases. We have to introduce a separate model for each use case and map between this model and our entities.

But use case-specific models allow for a crisp understanding of a use case, making it easier to maintain in the long run. Also, they allow multiple developers to work on different use cases in parallel without stepping on each other's toes.

Together with tight input validation, use case-specific input and output models go a long way toward a maintainable codebase.

5

Implementing a Web Adapter

Most applications today have some kind of web interface – either a UI that we can interact with via a web browser or an HTTP API that other systems can call to interact with our application.

In our target architecture, all communication with the outside world goes through adapters. So, let's discuss how we can implement an adapter that provides such a web interface.

Dependency Inversion

The following figure gives a zoomed-in view of the architectural elements that are relevant to our discussion of a web adapter—the adapter itself and the ports through which it interacts with our application core:

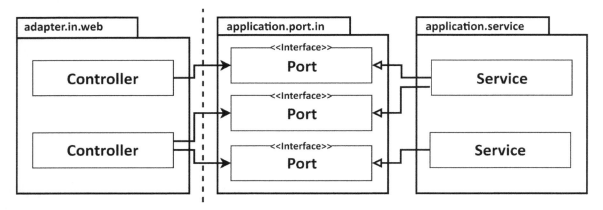

Figure 5.1: An incoming adapter talks to the application layer through dedicated incoming ports, which are interfaces implemented by the application services

The web adapter is a "driving" or "incoming" adapter. It takes requests from the outside and translates them into calls to our application core, telling it what to do. The control flow goes from the controllers in the web adapter to the services in the application layer.

The application layer provides specific ports through which the web adapter can communicate. The services implement these ports and the web adapter can call these ports.

If we look closer, we notice that this is the **Dependency Inversion Principle** in action. Since the control flow goes from left to right, we could just as well let the web adapter call the use cases directly, as shown in the following figure:

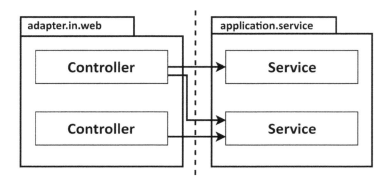

Figure 5.2: We can remove the port interfaces and call the services directly

So, why do we add another layer of indirection between the adapter and the use cases? The reason is that the ports are a specification of the places where the outside world can interact with our application core. Having ports in place, we know exactly what communication with the outside world takes place, which is valuable information for any maintenance engineer working on your legacy codebase.

Having said that, one of the shortcuts we will talk about in *Chapter 11, Taking Shortcuts Consciously*, is just leaving the incoming ports out and calling the application services directly.

One question remains, though, which is relevant for highly interactive applications. Imagine an application that sends real-time data to the user's browser via web sockets. How does the application core send this real-time data to the web adapter, which in turn sends it to the user's browser?

For this scenario, we definitely need a port. This port must be implemented by the web adapter and called by the application core, as depicted in the following figure:

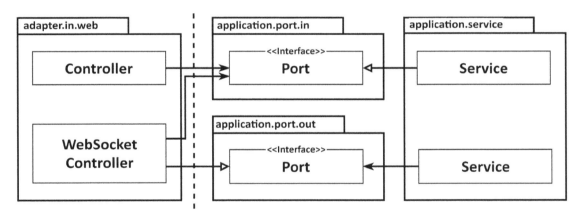

Figure 5.3: If an application must actively notify a web adapter, we need to go through an outgoing port to keep the dependencies in the right direction

Technically speaking, this would be an outgoing port and make the web adapter an incoming *and* outgoing adapter. But there is no reason that the same adapter cannot be both at the same time.

For the rest of this chapter, we will assume that the web adapter is an incoming adapter only since this is the most common case.

Responsibilities of a Web Adapter

What does a web adapter actually do? Let's say we want to provide a REST API for our BuckPal application. Where do the responsibilities of the web adapter start and where do they end?

A web adapter usually does these things:

1. Maps HTTP requests to Java objects

2. Performs authorization checks

3. Validates input

4. Maps input to the input model of the use case

5. Calls the use case

6. Maps the output of the use case back to HTTP

7. Returns an HTTP response

First of all, a web adapter must listen to HTTP requests that match certain criteria, such as a certain URL path, HTTP method, or content type. The parameters and the content of a matching HTTP request must then be deserialized into objects we can work with.

Commonly, a web adapter then does an authentication and authorization check and returns an error if it fails.

The state of the incoming objects can then be validated. But haven't we already discussed input validation as a responsibility of the input model to the use cases? Yes, the input model to the use cases should only allow input that is valid in the context of the use cases. But here, we are talking about the input model to the *web adapter*. It might have a completely different structure and semantics from the input model to the *use cases*, so we might have to perform different validations.

I don't advocate implementing the same validations in the web adapter as we have already done in the input model of the use cases. Instead, we should validate that *we can transform the input model of the web adapter into the input model of the use cases*. Anything that prevents us from doing this transformation is a validation error.

This brings us to the next responsibility of a web adapter: to call a certain use case with the transformed input model. The adapter then takes the output of the use case and serializes it into an HTTP response, which is sent back to the caller.

If anything goes wrong on the way and an exception is thrown, the web adapter must translate the error into a message that is sent back to the caller.

That's a lot of responsibilities weighing on the shoulders of our web adapter. But it's also a lot of responsibilities that the application layer should not be concerned with. Anything that has to do with HTTP must not leak into the application layer. If the application core knows that we are dealing with HTTP on the outside, we have essentially lost the option to perform the same domain logic from other incoming adapters that do not use HTTP. In a good architecture, we want to keep our options open.

Note that this boundary between the web adapter and application layer comes naturally if we start development with the domain and application layers instead of with the web layer. If we implement the use cases first, without thinking about any specific incoming adapter, we are not tempted to blur the boundary.

Slicing Controllers

In most web frameworks – such as Spring MVC in the Java world – we create controller classes, which perform the responsibilities we have discussed previously. So, do we build a single controller that answers all the requests directed at our application? We don't have to. A web adapter can certainly consist of more than one class.

We should take care, however, to put these classes into the same package hierarchy to mark them as belonging together, as discussed in *Chapter 3, Organizing Code*.

So, how many controllers do we build? I say we should build too many rather than too few. We should make sure that each controller implements a slice of the web adapter that is as narrow as possible and that shares as little as possible with other controllers.

Let's take the operations on an account entity within our BuckPal application. A popular approach is to create a single **AccountController** that accepts requests for all operations that relate to accounts. A Spring controller providing a REST API might look like the following code snippet:

```
package buckpal.adapter.web;


@RestController
@RequiredArgsConstructor
class AccountController {

  private final GetAccountBalanceQuery getAccountBalanceQuery;
  private final ListAccountsQuery listAccountsQuery;
  private final LoadAccountQuery loadAccountQuery;

  private final SendMoneyUseCase sendMoneyUseCase;
  private final CreateAccountUseCase createAccountUseCase;

  @GetMapping("/accounts")
  List<AccountResource> listAccounts(){
    ...
```

```
  }

  @GetMapping("/accounts/id")
  AccountResource getAccount(@PathVariable("accountId") Long accountId){

    ...

  }

  @GetMapping("/accounts/{id}/balance")
  long getAccountBalance(@PathVariable("accountId") Long accountId){

    ...

  }

  @PostMapping("/accounts")
  AccountResource createAccount(@RequestBody AccountResource account){

    ...

  }

  @PostMapping("/accounts/send/{sourceAccountId}/{targetAccountId}/{amount}")
  void sendMoney(
      @PathVariable("sourceAccountId") Long sourceAccountId,
      @PathVariable("targetAccountId") Long targetAccountId,
      @PathVariable("amount") Long amount) {

    ...

  }
}
```

Everything concerning the account resource is in a single class, which feels good. But let's discuss the downsides of this approach.

First, less code per class is a good thing. I have worked on a legacy project where the largest class had 30,000 lines of code. It was actually a conscious architecture decision (by our predecessors, mind you) that lead to there being 30,000 lines in a single class: to change the system at runtime, without re-deployment, it allowed us to upload compiled Java bytecode in a .class file. And it only allowed us to upload a single file, so this file had to contain all the code... .

That's no fun. Even if the controller only accumulates 200 lines of code over the years, it's still harder to grasp than 50 lines, even when it's cleanly separated into methods.

The same argument is valid for test code. If the controller itself has a lot of code, there will be a lot of test code. And, often, test code is even harder to grasp than production code, because it tends to be more abstract. We also want to make the tests for a certain piece of production code easy to find, which is easier in small classes.

What's equally important, however, is that putting all operations into a single controller class encourages the reuse of data structures. In the preceding code example, many operations share the **AccountResource** model class. It serves as a bucket for everything that is needed in any of the operations. **AccountResource** probably has an **id** field. This is not needed in the **create** operation and will probably cause confusion here more than it will help. Imagine that an **Account** has a one-to-many relationship with **User** objects. Do we include those **User** objects when creating or updating a book? Will the users be returned by the **list** operation? This is a simple example, but in any above-playsize project, we will ask these questions at some point.

So, I advocate the approach of creating a separate controller, potentially in a separate package, for each operation. Also, we should name the methods and classes as closely to our use cases as possible:

```
package buckpal.adapter.web;


@RestController
@RequiredArgsConstructor
public class SendMoneyController {

  private final SendMoneyUseCase;
```

```
@PostMapping("/accounts/send/{sourceAccountId}/{targetAccountId}/{amount}")
void sendMoney(
    @PathVariable("sourceAccountId") Long sourceAccountId,
    @PathVariable("targetAccountId") Long targetAccountId,
    @PathVariable("amount") Long amount) {

  SendMoneyCommand command = new SendMoneyCommand(
      new AccountId(sourceAccountId),
      new AccountId(targetAccountId),
      Money.of(amount));

  sendMoneyUseCase.sendMoney(command);
}


}
```

Also, each controller can have its own model, such as **CreateAccountResource** or **UpdateAccountResource**, or use primitives as input, as in the preceding example.

Those specialized model classes may even be private to the controller's package so they cannot accidentally be reused somewhere else. Controllers may still share models but using shared classes from another package makes us think about it more, and perhaps we will find out that we don't need half of the fields and create our own, after all.

Also, we should think hard about the names of the controllers and services. Instead of **CreateAccount**, for instance, wouldn't **RegisterAccount** be a better name? In our BuckPal application, the only way to create an account is for a user to register one. So, we use the word "register" in class names to better convey their meaning. There are certainly cases where the usual suspects **Create...**, **Update...**, and **Delete...** sufficiently describe a use case, but we might want to think twice before actually using them.

Another benefit of this slicing style is that it makes parallel work on different operations a breeze. We won't have merge conflicts if two developers work on different operations.

How Does This Help Me Build Maintainable Software?

When building a web adapter for an application, we should keep in mind that we are building an adapter that translates HTTP to method calls for the use cases of our application and translates the results back to HTTP and does not do any domain logic.

The application layer, on the other hand, should not do HTTP, so we should make sure not to leak HTTP details. This makes the web adapter replaceable by another adapter should the need arise.

When slicing web controllers, we should not be afraid to build many small classes that don't share a model. They are easier to grasp, to test, and support parallel work. It's more work initially to set up such fine-grained controllers, but it will pay off during maintenance.

Implementing a Persistence Adapter

In *Chapter 1, What's Wrong with Layers?*, I ranted about the traditional layered architecture and claimed that it supports "database-driven design" because, in the end, everything depends on the persistence layer. In this chapter, we will have a look at how to make the persistence layer a plugin to the application layer to invert this dependency.

Dependency Inversion

Instead of a persistence layer, we will talk about a persistence adapter that provides persistence functionality to the application services.

The following figure shows how we can apply the Dependency Inversion Principle to do just that:

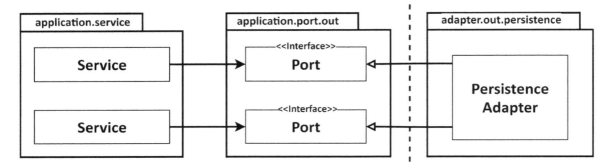

Figure 6.1: The services from the core use ports to access the persistence adapter

Our application services call port interfaces to access persistence functionality. These ports are implemented by a persistence adapter class that does the actual persistence work and is responsible for talking to the database.

In hexagonal architecture lingo, the persistence adapter is a "driven" or "outgoing" adapter, because it's called by our application and not the other way around.

The ports are effectively a layer of indirection between the application services and the persistence code. Let's remind ourselves that we are adding this layer of indirection in order to be able to evolve the domain code without having to think about persistence problems, meaning without code dependencies to the persistence layer. Refactoring the persistence code will not necessarily lead to a code change in the core.

Naturally, at runtime, we still have a dependency from our application core to the persistence adapter. If we modify code in the persistence layer and introduce a bug, for example, we may still break functionality in the application core. But as long as the contracts of the ports are fulfilled, we are free to do as we want in the persistence adapter without affecting the core.

The Responsibilities of a Persistence Adapter

Let's have a look at what a persistence adapter usually does:

1. Takes input

2. Maps input into a database format

3. Sends input to the database

4. Maps database output into an application format

5. Returns output

The persistence adapter takes input through a port interface. The input model may be a domain entity, or an object dedicated to a specific database operation, as specified by the interface.

It then maps the input model to a format it can work with to modify or query the database. In Java projects, we commonly use the Java Persistence API (JPA) to talk to a database, so we might map the input into JPA entity objects that reflect the structure of the database tables. Depending on the context, mapping the input model into JPA entities may be a lot of work for little gain, so we will talk about strategies without mapping in *Chapter 8, Mapping between Boundaries*.

Instead of using JPA or another object-relational mapping framework, we could use any other technique to talk to the database. We might map the input model to plain SQL statements and send these statements to the database, or we might serialize incoming data into files and read them back from there.

The important part is that the input model to the persistence adapter lies within the application core and not within the persistence adapter itself so that changes in the persistence adapter don't affect the core.

Next, the persistence adapter queries the database and receives the query results.

Finally, it maps the database answer into the output model expected by the port and returns it. Again, it's important that the output model lies within the application core and not within the persistence adapter.

Aside from the fact that the input and output models lie in the application core instead of the persistence adapter itself, the responsibilities are not really different from those of a traditional persistence layer.

But implementing a persistence adapter as described previously will inevitably raise some questions that we probably wouldn't ask when implementing a traditional persistence layer because we are so used to the traditional way that we don't think about them.

Slicing Port Interfaces

One question that comes to mind when implementing services is how to slice the port interfaces that define the database operations available to the application core.

It's common practice to create a single repository interface that provides all database operations for a certain entity, as shown in the following figure:

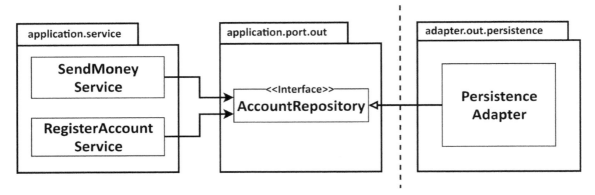

Figure 6.2: Centralizing all database operations into a single outgoing port interface makes all services depend on methods they don't need

Each service that relies on database operations will then have a dependency on this single "broad" port interface, even if it uses only a single method from the interface. This means we have unnecessary dependencies in our codebase.

Dependencies on methods that we don't need in our context make the code harder to understand and to test. Imagine we are writing a unit test for **RegisterAccountService** from the preceding figure. Which of the methods of the **AccountRepository** interface do we have to create a mock for? We have to first find out which of the **AccountRepository** methods the service actually calls. Having mocked only part of the interface may lead to other problems because the next person working on that test might expect the interface to be completely mocked and run into errors. So, they (again) will have to do some research.

To put it in the words of Martin C. Robert:

> *"Depending on something that carries baggage that you don't need can cause you troubles that you didn't expect." (Clean Architecture by Robert C. Martin, page 86).*

The Interface Segregation Principle provides an answer to this problem. It states that broad interfaces should be split into specific ones so that clients only know the methods they need.

If we apply this to our outgoing ports, we might get the result shown in the following figure:

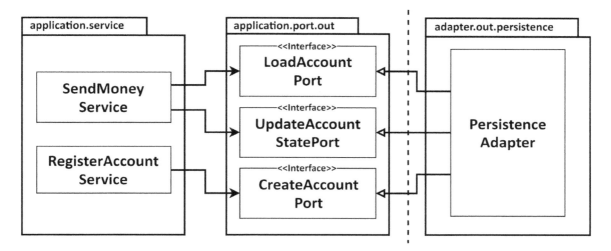

Figure 6.3: Applying the Interface Segregation Principle removes unnecessary dependencies and makes the existing dependencies more visible

Each service now only depends on the methods it actually needs. What's more, the names of the ports clearly state what they are about. In a test, we no longer have to think about which methods to mock, since most of the time there is only one method per port.

Having very narrow ports like these makes coding a plug-and-play experience. When working on a service, we just "plug in" the ports we need; there's no baggage to carry around.

Of course, the "one method per port" approach may not be applicable in all circumstances. There may be groups of database operations that are so cohesive and often used together that we may want to bundle them together in a single interface.

Slicing Persistence Adapters

In the preceding figures, we have seen a single persistence adapter class that implements all persistence ports. There is no rule, however, that forbids us to create more than one class, as long as all persistence ports are implemented.

We might choose, for instance, to implement one persistence adapter per domain class for which we need persistence operations (or "aggregate" in DDD lingo), as shown in the following figure:

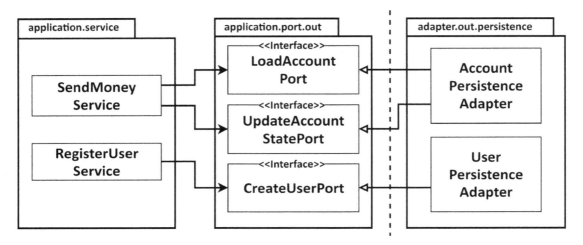

Figure 6.4: We can create multiple persistence adapters, one for each aggregate

This way, our persistence adapters are automatically sliced along the seams of the domain that we support with persistence functionality.

We might split our persistence adapters into even more classes, for instance, when we want to implement a couple of persistence ports using JPA or another OR-Mapper and some other ports using plain SQL for better performance. We might then create one JPA adapter and one plain SQL adapter, each implementing a subset of the persistence ports.

Remember that our domain code doesn't care about which class ultimately fulfills the contracts defined by the persistence ports. We are free to do as we see fit in the persistence layer, as long as all ports are implemented.

The "one persistence adapter per aggregate" approach is also a good foundation for separating the persistence needs for multiple bounded contexts in the future. Say, after a time, we identify a bounded context responsible for billing use cases. The following figure gives an overview of this scenario:

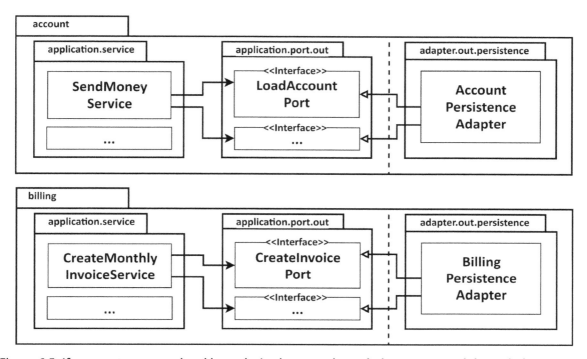

Figure 6.5: If we want to create hard boundaries between bounded contexts, each bounded context should have its own persistence adapter(s)

Each bounded context has its own persistence adapter (or potentially more than one, as described previously). The term "bounded context" implies boundaries, which means that services of the **account** context may not access persistence adapters of the **billing** context and vice versa. If one context needs something from the other context, it can access it via a dedicated incoming port.

Example with Spring Data JPA

Let's have a look at a code example that implements **AccountPersistenceAdapter** from the preceding figures. This adapter will have to save and load accounts to and from the database. We saw the **Account** entity in *Chapter 4, Implementing a Use Case*, but here is its skeleton again for reference:

```
package buckpal.domain;


@AllArgsConstructor(access = AccessLevel.PRIVATE)

public class Account {

  @Getter private final AccountId id;

  @Getter private final ActivityWindow activityWindow;
```

```java
    private final Money baselineBalance;

    public static Account withoutId(
            Money baselineBalance,
            ActivityWindow activityWindow) {
        return new Account(null, baselineBalance, activityWindow);
    }

    public static Account withId(
            AccountId accountId,
            Money baselineBalance,
            ActivityWindow activityWindow) {
        return new Account(accountId, baselineBalance, activityWindow);
    }

    public Money calculateBalance() {
        // ...
    }

    public boolean withdraw(Money money, AccountId targetAccountId) {
        // ...
    }

    public boolean deposit(Money money, AccountId sourceAccountId) {
        // ...
    }

}
```

Note that the **Account** class is not a simple data class with getters and setters but instead tries to be as immutable as possible. It only provides factory methods that create an **Account** entity in a valid state and all mutating methods perform some validation, such as checking the account balance before withdrawing money, so that we cannot create an invalid domain model.

We will use Spring Data JPA to talk to the database, so we also need `@Entity`-annotated classes representing the database state of an account:

```
package buckpal.adapter.persistence;


@Entity
@Table(name = "account")
@Data
@AllArgsConstructor
@NoArgsConstructor
class AccountJpaEntity {


    @Id
    @GeneratedValue
    private Long id;


}
```

The code block for the **activity** table:

```
package buckpal.adapter.persistence;


@Entity
@Table(name = "activity")
@Data
@AllArgsConstructor
@NoArgsConstructor
class ActivityJpaEntity {

    @Id
    @GeneratedValue
    private Long id;

    @Column private LocalDateTime timestamp;
    @Column private Long ownerAccountId;
```

```
@Column private Long sourceAccountId;

@Column private Long targetAccountId;

@Column private Long amount;

}
```

The state of an account consists merely of an ID at this stage. Later, additional fields such as user ID may be added. More interesting is **ActivityJpaEntity**, which contains all activities for a specific account. We could have connected **ActivityJpaEntity** with **AccountJpaEntity** via JPA's **@ManyToOne** or **@OneToMany** annotations to mark the relation between them, but we have opted to leave this out for now, as it adds side effects to database queries. In fact, at this stage, it would probably be easier to use a simpler ORM than JPA to implement the persistence adapter, but we will use it anyway because we think we might need it in the future.

Does that sound familiar to you? You choose JPA as an OR mapper because it's the thing people use for this problem. A couple months into development you curse eager and lazy loading and the caching features and wish for something simpler. JPA is a great tool, but for many problems, simpler solutions may be, well, simpler.

Next, we use Spring Data to create repository interfaces that provide basic CRUD functionality out of the box, as well as custom queries to load certain activities from the database:

```
interface AccountRepository extends JpaRepository<AccountJpaEntity, Long> {

}
```

And here's the code for the **ActivityRepository**:

```
interface ActivityRepository extends JpaRepository<ActivityJpaEntity, Long>
{

  @Query("select a from ActivityJpaEntity a " +
      "where a.ownerAccountId = :ownerAccountId " +
      "and a.timestamp >= :since")
  List<ActivityJpaEntity> findByOwnerSince(
      @Param("ownerAccountId") Long ownerAccountId,
      @Param("since") LocalDateTime since);


  @Query("select sum(a.amount) from ActivityJpaEntity a " +
      "where a.targetAccountId = :accountId " +
```

```
        "and a.ownerAccountId = :accountId " +
        "and a.timestamp < :until")
    Long getDepositBalanceUntil(
        @Param("accountId") Long accountId,
        @Param("until") LocalDateTime until);


    @Query("select sum(a.amount) from ActivityJpaEntity a " +
        "where a.sourceAccountId = :accountId " +
        "and a.ownerAccountId = :accountId " +
        "and a.timestamp < :until")
    Long getWithdrawalBalanceUntil(
        @Param("accountId") Long accountId,
        @Param("until") LocalDateTime until);


}
```

Spring Boot will automatically find these repositories, and Spring Data will work its magic to provide an implementation behind the repository interface that will actually talk to the database.

Now that we have JPA entities and repositories in place, we can implement the persistence adapter that provides the persistence functionality for our application:

```
@RequiredArgsConstructor
@Component
class AccountPersistenceAdapter implements
        LoadAccountPort,
        UpdateAccountStatePort {

    private final AccountRepository accountRepository;
    private final ActivityRepository activityRepository;
    private final AccountMapper accountMapper;

    @Override
    public Account loadAccount(
```

```
            AccountId accountId,
            LocalDateTime baselineDate) {

    AccountJpaEntity account =
        accountRepository.findById(accountId.getValue())
            .orElseThrow(EntityNotFoundException::new);

    List<ActivityJpaEntity> activities =
        activityRepository.findByOwnerSince(
            accountId.getValue(),
            baselineDate);

    Long withdrawalBalance = orZero(activityRepository
        .getWithdrawalBalanceUntil(
            accountId.getValue(),
            baselineDate));

    Long depositBalance = orZero(activityRepository
        .getDepositBalanceUntil(
            accountId.getValue(),
            baselineDate));

    return accountMapper.mapToDomainEntity(
        account,
        activities,
        withdrawalBalance,
        depositBalance);

}

private Long orZero(Long value){
  return value == null ? 0L : value;
```

```
  }

  @Override
  public void updateActivities(Account account) {
    for (Activity activity : account.getActivityWindow().getActivities()) {
      if (activity.getId() == null) {
        activityRepository.save(accountMapper.mapToJpaEntity(activity));
      }
    }
  }


}
```

The persistence adapter implements two ports that are needed by the application, **LoadAccountPort**, and **UpdateAccountStatePort**.

To load an account from the database, we load it from **AccountRepository** and then load the activities of this account for a certain time window through **ActivityRepository**.

To create a valid **Account** domain entity, we also need the balance the account had before the start of this activity window, so we get the sum of all withdrawals and deposits for this account from the database. Finally, we map all this data to an **Account** domain entity and return it to the caller.

To update the state of an account, we iterate all the activities of the **Account** entity and check whether they have IDs. If they don't, they are new activities, which we persist through **ActivityRepository**.

In the scenario described previously, we have a two-way mapping between the **Account** and **Activity** domain models and the **AccountJpaEntity** and **ActivityJpaEntity** database models. Why make the effort of mapping back and forth? Couldn't we just move the JPA annotations to the **Account** and **Activity** classes and directly store them as entities in the database?

Such a "no mapping" strategy may be a valid choice, as we will see in *Chapter 8, Mapping between Boundaries*, when we will be talking about mapping strategies. However, JPA then forces us to make compromises in the domain model. For instance, JPA requires entities to have a no-args constructor. Or it might be that, in the persistence layer, a **@ManyToOne** relationship makes sense from a performance point of view, but in the domain model we want this relationship to be the other way around because we always only load part of the data anyway.

So, if we want to create a rich domain model without compromising the underlying persistence, we will have to map between the domain model and the persistence model.

What about Database Transactions?

We have not touched upon the topic of database transactions yet. Where do we put our transaction boundaries?

A transaction should span all write operations to the database that are performed within a certain use case so that all those operations can be rolled back together if one of them fails.

Since the persistence adapter doesn't know which other database operations are part of the same use case, it cannot decide when to open and close a transaction. We have to delegate this responsibility to the services that orchestrate the calls to the persistence adapter.

The easiest way to do this with Java and Spring is to add the **@Transactional** annotation to the application service classes so that Spring will wrap all public methods with a transaction:

```
package buckpal.application.service;


@Transactional
public class SendMoneyService implements SendMoneyUseCase {

  ...

}
```

If we want our services to stay pure and not be stained with **@Transactional** annotations, we can use aspect-oriented programming – for example, with AspectJ – in order to weave transaction boundaries into our codebase.

How Does This Help Me Build Maintainable Software?

Building a persistence adapter that acts as a plugin to the domain code frees the domain code from persistence details so that we can build a rich domain model.

Using narrow port interfaces, we have the flexibility to implement one port this way and another port that way, perhaps even with a different persistence technology, without the application noticing. We can even switch out the complete persistence layer, as long as the port contracts are obeyed.

Testing Architecture Elements

In many projects I have witnessed, automated testing is a mystery. Everyone writes tests as they see fit because it's required by some dusty rule documented in a wiki, but no one can answer targeted questions about the team's testing strategy.

This chapter provides a testing strategy for hexagonal architecture. For each element of our architecture, we will discuss the type of test to cover it.

The Test Pyramid

Let's start the discussion about testing along the lines of the test pyramid (*the test pyramid can be traced back to Mike Cohn's book "Succeeding with Agile" from 2009*) in the following figure, which is a metaphor that helps us to decide how many tests and of which type we should aim for:

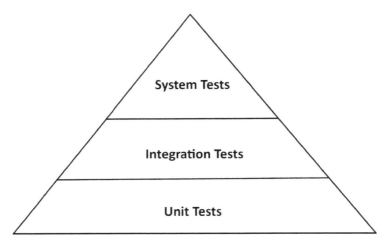

Figure 7.1: According to the test pyramid, we should create many cheap tests and fewer expensive ones

The basic statement is that we should have high coverage of fine-grained tests that are cheap to build, easy to maintain, fast-running, and stable. These are unit tests verifying that a single "unit" (usually a class) works as expected.

Once tests combine multiple units and cross-unit boundaries, architectural boundaries, or even system boundaries, they tend to become more expensive to build, slower to run, and more brittle (failing due to some configuration error instead of a functional error). The pyramid tells us that the more expensive those tests become, the less we should aim for high coverage of those tests because otherwise we will spend too much time building tests instead of new functionality.

Depending on the context, the test pyramid is often shown with different layers. Let's take a look at the layers I chose to discuss testing our hexagonal architecture. Note that the definitions of "unit test," "integration test," and "system test" vary with context. In one project, they may mean a different thing than in another. The following are interpretations of these terms as we will use them in this chapter.

Unit tests are the base of the pyramid. A unit test usually instantiates a single class and tests its functionality through its interface. If the class under test has dependencies to other classes, those other classes are not instantiated, but replaced with mocks, simulating the behavior of the real classes as needed during the test.

Integration tests form the next layer of the pyramid. These tests instantiate a network of multiple units and verify whether this network works as expected by sending some data into it through the interface of an entry class. In our interpretation, integration tests will cross the boundary between two layers, so the network of objects is not complete or must work against mocks at some point.

System tests, finally, spin up the whole network of objects that makes up our application and verify whether a certain use case works as expected through all the layers of the application.

Above the system tests, there might be a layer of end-to-end tests that include the UI of the application. We will not consider end-to-end tests here since we are only discussing backend architecture in this book.

Now that we have defined some test types, let's see which type of test best fits each of the layers of our hexagonal architecture.

Testing a Domain Entity with Unit Tests

We will start by looking at a domain entity at the center of our architecture. Let's recall the **Account** entity from *Chapter 4, Implementing a Use Case*. The state of an **Account** consists of a balance the account had at a certain point in the past (the baseline balance) and a list of deposits and withdrawals (activities) since then. We now want to verify that the `withdraw()` method works as expected:

```
class AccountTest {


  @Test
  void withdrawalSucceeds() {
    AccountId accountId = new AccountId(1L);
    Account account = defaultAccount()
        .withAccountId(accountId)
        .withBaselineBalance(Money.of(555L))
        .withActivityWindow(new ActivityWindow(
            defaultActivity()
                .withTargetAccount(accountId)
                .withMoney(Money.of(999L)).build(),
            defaultActivity()
                .withTargetAccount(accountId)
                .withMoney(Money.of(1L)).build()))
```

```
        .build();

    boolean success = account.withdraw(Money.of(555L), new AccountId(99L));

    assertThat(success).isTrue();
    assertThat(account.getActivityWindow().getActivities()).hasSize(3);
    assertThat(account.calculateBalance()).isEqualTo(Money.of(1000L));
  }
}
```

The preceding test is a plain unit test that instantiates **Account** in a specific state, calls its **withdraw()** method, and verifies that the withdrawal was successful and had the expected side effects on the state of the **Account** object under test.

The test is rather easy to set up, easy to understand, and it runs very quickly. Tests don't come much simpler than this. Unit tests like this are our best bet to verify the business rules encoded within our domain entities. We don't need any other type of test since domain entity behavior has little to no dependencies on other classes.

Testing a Use Case with Unit Tests

Going a layer outward, the next architecture element to test is the use cases. Let's look at a test of **SendMoneyService**, discussed in *Chapter 4, Implementing a Use Case*. The **SendMoney** use case locks the source **Account** so no other transactions can change its balance in the meantime. If we can successfully withdraw money from the source account, we lock the target account as well and deposit the money there. Finally, we unlock both accounts again.

We want to verify that everything works as expected when the transaction succeeds:

```
class SendMoneyServiceTest {

  // declaration of fields omitted

  @Test
  void transactionSucceeds() {

    Account sourceAccount = givenSourceAccount();
```

```java
    Account targetAccount = givenTargetAccount();

    givenWithdrawalWillSucceed(sourceAccount);
    givenDepositWillSucceed(targetAccount);

    Money money = Money.of(500L);

    SendMoneyCommand command = new SendMoneyCommand(
        sourceAccount.getId(),
        targetAccount.getId(),
        money);

    boolean success = sendMoneyService.sendMoney(command);

    assertThat(success).isTrue();

    AccountId sourceAccountId = sourceAccount.getId();
    AccountId targetAccountId = targetAccount.getId();

    then(accountLock).should().lockAccount(eq(sourceAccountId));
    then(sourceAccount).should().withdraw(eq(money), eq(targetAccountId));
    then(accountLock).should().releaseAccount(eq(sourceAccountId));

    then(accountLock).should().lockAccount(eq(targetAccountId));
    then(targetAccount).should().deposit(eq(money), eq(sourceAccountId));
    then(accountLock).should().releaseAccount(eq(targetAccountId));

    thenAccountsHaveBeenUpdated(sourceAccountId, targetAccountId);
  }

  // helper methods omitted
}
```

To make the test a little more readable, it's structured into given/when/then sections, which are commonly used in behavior-driven development.

In the "given" section, we create the source and target **Account** instance and put them into the correct state with some methods whose names start with **given...()**. We also create an instance of **SendMoneyCommand** to act as input to the use case. In the "when" section, we simply call the **sendMoney()** method to invoke the use cases. The "then" section asserts that the transaction was successful and verifies that certain methods have been called on the source and target **Account** and on the **AccountLock** instance, which is responsible for locking and unlocking the accounts.

Under the hood, the test makes use of the Mockito libary (https://site.mockito.org/) library to create mock objects in the **given...()** methods. Mockito also provides the **then()** method to verify whether a certain method has been called on a mock object.

Since the use case service under test is stateless, we cannot verify a certain state in the "then" section. Instead, the test verifies that the service interacted with certain methods on its (mocked) dependencies. This means that the test is vulnerable to changes in the *structure* of the code under test and not only its *behavior*. This, in turn, means that there is a higher chance that the test has to be modified if the code under test is refactored.

With this in mind, we should think hard about which interactions we actually want to verify in the test. It might be a good idea not to verify *all* interactions as we did in the preceding test but instead focus on the most important ones. Otherwise, we have to change the test with every single change to the class under test, undermining the value of the test.

While this test is still a unit test, it borders on being an integration test, because we are testing the interaction of dependencies. It's easier to create and maintain than a full-blown integration test, however, because we are working with mocks and don't have to manage the real dependencies.

Testing a Web Adapter with Integration Tests

Moving outward another layer, we arrive at our adapters. Let's discuss testing a web adapter.

Recall that a web adapter takes input, for example, in the form of JSON strings, via HTTP, maybe does some validation on it, maps the input to the format a use case expects, and then passes it to that use case. It then maps the result of the use case back to JSON and returns it to the client via an HTTP response.

In the test for a web adapter, we want to make certain that all those steps work as expected:

```
@WebMvcTest(controllers = SendMoneyController.class)
class SendMoneyControllerTest {

  @Autowired
  private MockMvc mockMvc;

  @MockBean
  private SendMoneyUseCase sendMoneyUseCase;

  @Test
  void testSendMoney() throws Exception {

    mockMvc.perform(
        post("/accounts/send/{sourceAccountId}/{targetAccountId}/{amount}",
            41L, 42L, 500)
          .header("Content-Type", "application/json"))
          .andExpect(status().isOk());

    then(sendMoneyUseCase).should()
        .sendMoney(eq(new SendMoneyCommand(
            new AccountId(41L),
            new AccountId(42L),
            Money.of(500L))));
  }

}
```

The preceding test is a standard integration test for a web controller named **SendMoneyController** built with the Spring Boot framework. In the **testSendMoney()** method, we create an input object and then send a mock HTTP request to the web controller. The request body contains the input object as a JSON string.

With the **isOk()** method, we then verify that the status of the HTTP response is **200** and we verify that the mocked use case class has been called.

Most of the responsibilities of a web adapter are covered by this test.

We are not actually testing over the HTTP protocol since we are mocking that away with the **MockMvc** object. We trust that the framework translates everything to and from HTTP properly; there's no need to test the framework.

The whole path from mapping the input from JSON into a **SendMoneyCommand** object is covered, however. If we built the **SendMoneyCommand** object as a self-validating command, as explained in *Chapter 4, Implementing a Use Case*, we have even made sure that this mapping produces syntactically valid input for the use case. Also, we have verified that the use case is actually called and that the HTTP response has the expected status.

So, why is this an integration test and not a unit test? Even though it seems that we are only testing a single web controller class in this test, there's a lot more going on under the covers. With the **@WebMvcTest** annotation, we tell Spring to instantiate a whole network of objects that is responsible for responding to certain request paths, the mapping between Java and JSON, validating HTTP input, and so on. And in this test, we are verifying that our web controller works as a part of this network.

Since the web controller is heavily bound to the Spring framework, it makes sense to test it integrated into this framework instead of testing it in isolation. If we tested the web controller with a plain unit test, we'd lose coverage of all the mapping and validation and HTTP stuff and we could never be sure whether it actually worked in production, where it's just a cog in the machine of the framework.

Testing a Persistence Adapter with Integration Tests

For a similar reason, it makes sense to cover persistence adapters with integration tests instead of unit tests, since we not only want to verify the logic within the adapter, but also the mapping into the database.

We want to test the persistence adapter we built in *Chapter 6, Implementing a Persistence Adapter*. The adapter has two methods, one for loading an **Account** entity from the database and another to save new account activities to the database:

```
@DataJpaTest

@Import({AccountPersistenceAdapter.class, AccountMapper.class})
```

```java
class AccountPersistenceAdapterTest {

  @Autowired
  private AccountPersistenceAdapter adapterUnderTest;

  @Autowired
  private ActivityRepository activityRepository;

  @Test
  @Sql("AccountPersistenceAdapterTest.sql")
  void loadsAccount() {
    Account account = adapter.loadAccount(
        new AccountId(1L),
        LocalDateTime.of(2018, 8, 10, 0, 0));

    assertThat(account.getActivityWindow().getActivities()).hasSize(2);
    assertThat(account.calculateBalance()).isEqualTo(Money.of(500));
  }

  @Test
  void updatesActivities() {
    Account account = defaultAccount()
        .withBaselineBalance(Money.of(555L))
        .withActivityWindow(new ActivityWindow(
            defaultActivity()
                .withId(null)
                .withMoney(Money.of(1L)).build()))
        .build();

    adapter.updateActivities(account);
```

```
        assertThat(activityRepository.count()).isEqualTo(1);


        ActivityJpaEntity savedActivity = activityRepository.findAll().get(0);
        assertThat(savedActivity.getAmount()).isEqualTo(1L);
    }


}
```

With **@DataJpaTest**, we are telling Spring to instantiate the network of objects that are needed for database access, including our Spring Data repositories that connect to the database. We add an additional **@Import** statement to make sure that certain objects are added to that network. These objects are needed by the adapter under test to map incoming domain objects to database objects, for instance.

In the test for the **loadAccount()** method, we put the database into a certain state using a SQL script. Then, we simply load the account through the adapter API and verify that it has the state that we would expect it to have given the database state in the SQL script.

The test for **updateActivities()** goes the other way around. We create an **Account** object with new account activity and pass it to the adapter to persist. Then, we check whether the activity has been saved to the database through the API of **ActivityRepository**.

An important aspect of these tests is that we are not mocking away the database. The tests are actually hitting the database. Had we mocked the database away, the tests would still cover the same lines of code, producing the same high coverage of lines of code. But despite this high coverage, the tests would still have a rather high chance of failing in a setup with a real database due to errors in SQL statements or unexpected mapping errors between database tables and Java objects.

Note that, by default, Spring will spin up an in-memory database to use during tests. This is very practical, as we don't have to configure anything, and the tests will work out of the box.

Since this in-memory database is most probably not the database we are using in production, however, there is still a significant chance of something going wrong with the real database even when the tests worked perfectly against the in-memory database. Databases love to implement their own flavor of SQL, for instance.

For this reason, persistence adapter tests should run against the real database. Libraries such as Testcontainers (https://www.testcontainers.org/) are a great help in this regard, spinning up a Docker container with a database on demand.

Running against the real database has the added benefit that we don't have to take care of two different database systems. If we are using the in-memory database during tests, we might have to configure it in a certain way, or we might have to create separate versions of database migration scripts for each database, which is no fun at all.

Testing Main Paths with System Tests

On top of the pyramid of system tests, a system test starts up the whole application and runs requests against its API, verifying that all our layers work in concert.

In a system test for the "Send Money" use case, we send an HTTP request to the application and validate the response as well as the new balance of the account:

```
@SpringBootTest(webEnvironment = WebEnvironment.RANDOM_PORT)
class SendMoneySystemTest {

  @Autowired
  private TestRestTemplate restTemplate;

  @Test
  @Sql("SendMoneySystemTest.sql")
  void sendMoney() {

    Money initialSourceBalance = sourceAccount().calculateBalance();
    Money initialTargetBalance = targetAccount().calculateBalance();

    ResponseEntity response = whenSendMoney(
        sourceAccountId(),
        targetAccountId(),
        transferredAmount());

    then(response.getStatusCode())
        .isEqualTo(HttpStatus.OK);

    then(sourceAccount().calculateBalance())
```

```
            .isEqualTo(initialSourceBalance.minus(transferredAmount()));


    then(targetAccount().calculateBalance())
        .isEqualTo(initialTargetBalance.plus(transferredAmount()));


}


private ResponseEntity whenSendMoney(
    AccountId sourceAccountId,
    AccountId targetAccountId,
    Money amount) {


    HttpHeaders headers = new HttpHeaders();
    headers.add("Content-Type", "application/json");
    HttpEntity<Void> request = new HttpEntity<>(null, headers);


    return restTemplate.exchange(
        "/accounts/sendMoney/{sourceAccountId}/{targetAccountId}/{amount}",
        HttpMethod.POST,
        request,
        Object.class,
        sourceAccountId.getValue(),
        targetAccountId.getValue(),
        amount.getAmount());
}


    // some helper methods omitted
}
```

With @SpringBootTest, we are telling Spring to start up the whole network of objects that make up the application. We are also configuring the application to expose itself on a random port.

In the **test** method, we simply create a request, send it to the application, and then check the response status and the new balance of the accounts.

We are using **TestRestTemplate** to send the request and not **MockMvc**, as we did earlier in the web adapter test. This means we are doing real HTTP, bringing the test a little closer to a production environment.

Just as we are going over real HTTP, we are going through the real output adapters. In our case, this is only a persistence adapter that connects the application to a database. In an application that talks to other systems, we would have additional output adapters in place. It's not always feasible to have all those third-party systems up and running, even for a system test, so we might mock them away, after all. Our hexagonal architecture makes this as easy as it can be for us since we only have to stub out a couple of output port interfaces.

Note that I went out of my way to make the test as readable as possible. I hid every bit of ugly logic within helper methods. These methods now form a domain-specific language that we can use to verify the state of things.

While a domain-specific language like this is a good idea in any type of test, it's even more important in system tests. System tests simulate the real users of the application much better than a unit or integration test can, so we can use them to verify the application from the viewpoint of the user. This is much easier with a suitable vocabulary at hand. This vocabulary also enables domain experts, who are best suited to embody a user of the application and who probably aren't programmers, to reason about the tests and give feedback. There are whole libraries for behavior-driven development, such as JGiven (http://jgiven.org/), that provide a framework to create a vocabulary for your tests.

If we have created unit and integration tests as described in the previous sections, the system tests will cover a lot of the same code. Do they even provide any additional benefits? Yes, they do. Usually, they flush out other types of bugs than the unit and integration tests do. Some mapping between the layers could be off, for instance, which we would not notice with the unit and integration tests alone.

System tests play out their strengths best if they combine multiple use cases to create scenarios. Each scenario represents a certain path a user might typically take through the application. If the most important scenarios are covered by passing system tests, we can assume that we haven't broken the application with our latest modifications and it is ready to ship.

How Much Testing is Enough?

A question many project teams I have been part of couldn't answer is how much testing we should do. Is it enough if our tests cover 80% of our lines of code? Should it be higher than that?

Line coverage is a bad metric to measure test success. Any goal other than 100% is completely meaningless because important parts of the codebase might not be covered at all. And even at 100%, we still can't be sure that every bug has been squashed.

I suggest measuring test success by how comfortable we feel to ship the software. If we trust the tests enough to ship after having executed them, we are good. The more often we ship, the more trust we can have in our tests. If we only ship twice a year, no one will trust the tests because they will only prove themselves twice a year.

This requires a leap of faith the first couple of times we ship, but if we make it a priority to fix *and learn from* bugs in production, we are on the right track.

For each production bug, we should ask the question, "Why didn't our tests catch this bug?", document the answer, and then add a test that covers it. Over time, this will make us comfortable with shipping and the documentation will even provide a metric to gauge our improvement over time.

It helps, however, to start with a strategy that defines the tests we should create. One such strategy for our hexagonal architecture is this one:

* While implementing a domain entity, cover it with a unit test.
* While implementing a use case, cover it with a unit test.
* While implementing an adapter, cover it with an integration test.
* Cover the most important paths a user can take through the application with a system test.

Note the words "while implementing": when tests are done *during* the development of a feature and not *after*, they become a development tool and no longer feel like a chore.

If we have to spend an hour fixing tests each time we add a new field, however, we are doing something wrong. Probably, our tests are too vulnerable to structural changes in the code and we should look at how to improve that. Tests lose their value if we have to modify them for each refactoring.

How Does This Help Me Build Maintainable Software?

The **Hexagonal Architecture** style cleanly separates domain logic and outward-facing adapters. This helps us to define a clear testing strategy that covers the central domain logic with unit tests and the adapters with integration tests.

The input and output ports provide very visible mocking points in tests. For each port, we can decide to mock it or to use the real implementation. If the ports are each very small and focused, mocking them is a breeze instead of a chore. The fewer methods a port interface provides, the less confusion there is about which of the methods we have to mock in a test.

If it becomes too much of a burden to mock things away or if we don't know what kind of test we should use to cover a certain part of the code base, it's a warning sign. In this regard, our tests have the additional responsibility of acting as a canary – to warn us about flaws in the architecture and to steer us back on the path to creating a maintainable codebase.

Mapping Between Boundaries

In the previous chapters, we discussed the web, application, domain, and persistence layers and what each of those layers contributes to implementing a use case.

We have, however, barely touched upon the dreaded and omnipresent topic of mapping between the models of each layer. I bet you have had a discussion at some point about whether to use the same model in two layers in order to avoid implementing a mapper.

The argument might have gone something like this:

Pro-Mapping Developer:

If we don't map between layers, we have to use the same model in both layers, which means that the layers will be tightly coupled.

Contra-Mapping Developer:

*But if we **do** map between layers, we produce a lot of boilerplate code, which is overkill for many use cases, since they're only doing CRUD and have the same model across layers anyway.*

As is often the case in discussions like this, there's truth to both sides of the argument. Let's discuss some mapping strategies with their pros and cons and see whether we can help those developers make a decision.

The "No Mapping" Strategy

The first strategy is actually not mapping at all:

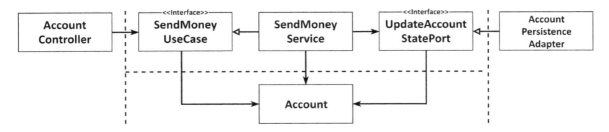

Figure 8.1: If the port interfaces use the domain model as the input and output model, we don't need to map between layers

The preceding figure shows the components that are relevant to the "Send Money" use case from our BuckPal example application.

In the web layer, the web controller calls the **SendMoneyUseCase** interface to execute the use case. This interface takes an **Account** object as an argument. This means that both the web layer and the application layer need access to the **Account** class – both are using the same model.

On the other side of the application, we have the same relationship between the persistence and application layers. Since all layers use the same model, we don't need to implement a mapping between them.

But what are the consequences of this design?

The web and persistence layers may have special requirements for their models. If our web layer exposes its model via REST, for instance, the model classes might need some annotations that define how to serialize certain fields into JSON. The same is true for the persistence layer if we are using an ORM framework, which might require some annotations that define the database mapping.

In the example, all of those special requirements have to be dealt with in the **Account** domain model class even though the domain and application layers are not interested in them. This violates the **Single Responsibility Principle** since the **Account** class has to be changed due to reasons related to the web, application, *and* persistence layers.

Aside from the technical requirements, each layer might require certain custom fields in the **Account** class. This might lead to a fragmented domain model with certain fields only relevant in one layer.

Does this mean, though, that we should never, ever, implement a "no mapping" strategy? Certainly not.

Even though it might feel dirty, a "no mapping" strategy can be perfectly valid.

Consider a simple CRUD use case. Do we really need to map the same fields from the web model into the domain model and from the domain model into the persistence model? I'd say we don't.

And what about those JSON or ORM annotations on the domain model? Do they really bother us? Even if we have to change an annotation or two in the domain model if something changes in the persistence layer, so what?

As long as all layers need exactly the same information in exactly the same structure, a "no mapping" strategy is a perfectly valid option.

However, as soon as we are dealing with web or persistence issues in the application or domain layer (aside from annotations, perhaps), we should move to another mapping strategy.

There is a lesson for the two developers from the introduction here: even though we have decided on a certain mapping strategy in the past, we can change it later.

In my experience, many use cases start their life as simple CRUD use cases. Later, they might grow into a full-fledged business use case with a rich behavior and validations that justify a more expensive mapping strategy. Or they might forever keep their CRUD status, in which case, we are glad that we haven't invested in a different mapping strategy.

The "Two-Way" Mapping Strategy

A mapping strategy where each layer has its own model is what I call the "two-way" mapping strategy, outlined in the following figure:

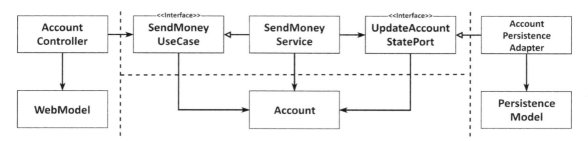

Figure 8.2: With each adapter having its own model, the adapters are responsible for mapping their model into the domain model and back

Each layer has its own model, which may have a structure that is completely different from the domain model.

The web layer maps the web model into the domain model that is expected by the incoming ports. It also maps domain objects returned by the incoming ports back into the web model.

The persistence layer is responsible for a similar mapping between the domain model, which is used by the outgoing ports, and the persistence model.

Both layers map in two directions, hence the name "two-way" mapping.

With each layer having its own model, each layer can modify its own model without affecting the other layers (as long as the contents are unchanged). The web model can have a structure that allows the optimal presentation of the data. The domain model can have a structure that best allows implementing the use cases. And the persistence model can have the structure needed by an ORM for persisting objects to a database.

This mapping strategy also leads to a clean domain model that is not dirtied by web or persistence concerns. It does not contain JSON or ORM mapping annotations. The single responsibility principle is satisfied.

Another bonus of "two-way" mapping is that, after the "no mapping" strategy, it's conceptually the simplest mapping strategy. The mapping responsibilities are clear: the outer layers/adapters map into the model of the inner layers and back. The inner layers only know their own model and can concentrate on the domain logic instead of mapping.

As with every mapping strategy, "two-way" mapping also has its drawbacks.

First of all, it usually results in a lot of boilerplate code. Even if we use one of the many mapping frameworks out there to reduce the amount of code, implementing the mapping between models usually takes up a good portion of our time. This is partly due to the fact that debugging mapping logic is a pain – especially when using a mapping framework that hides its inner workings behind a layer of generic code and reflection.

Another drawback is that the domain model is used to communicate across layer boundaries. The incoming ports and outgoing ports use domain objects as input parameters and return values. This makes them vulnerable to changes that are triggered by the needs of the outer layers, whereas it's desirable for the domain model only to evolve due to the needs of the domain logic.

Just like the "no mapping" strategy, the "two-way" mapping strategy is not a silver bullet. In many projects, however, this kind of mapping is considered a holy law that we have to comply with throughout the whole code base, even for the simplest CRUD use cases. This unnecessarily slows down development.

No mapping strategy shouldn't be considered an iron law. Instead, we should decide for each use case.

The "Full" Mapping Strategy

Another mapping strategy is what I call the "full" mapping strategy, sketched in the following figure:

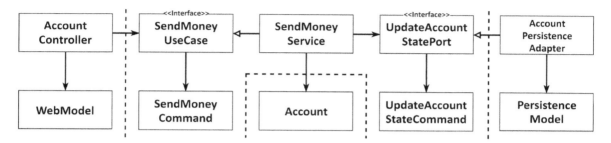

Figure 8.3: With each operation requiring its own model, the web adapter and application layer each map their model into the model expected by the operation they want to execute

This mapping strategy introduces a separate input and output model *per operation*. Instead of using the domain model to communicate across layer boundaries, we use a model specific to each operation, such as **SendMoneyCommand**, which acts as an input model to the **SendMoneyUseCase** port in the figure. We can call those models "commands," "requests," or something similar.

The web layer is responsible for mapping its input into the command object of the application layer. Such a command makes the interface to the application layer very explicit, with little room for interpretation. Each use case has its own command with its own fields and validations. There's no guessing involved as to which fields should be filled and which fields better be left empty since they would otherwise trigger a validation we don't want for our current use case.

The application layer is then responsible for mapping the command object into whatever it needs to modify the domain model according to the use case.

Naturally, mapping from one layer into many different commands requires even more mapping code than mapping between a single web model and a domain model. This mapping, however, is significantly easier to implement and maintain than a mapping that has to handle the needs of many use cases instead of only one.

I don't advocate this mapping strategy as a global pattern. It plays out its advantages best between the web layer (or any other incoming adapter) and the application layer to clearly demarcate the state-modifying use cases of the application. I would not use it between the application and persistence layer due to the mapping overhead.

Also, in some cases, I would restrict this kind of mapping to the input model of operations and simply use a domain object as the output model. **SendMoneyUseCase** might then return an **Account** object with the updated balance, for instance.

This shows that mapping strategies can and should be mixed. No mapping strategy needs to be a global rule across all layers.

The "One-Way" Mapping Strategy

There is yet another mapping strategy with another set of pros and cons – the "one-way" strategy sketched in the following figure:

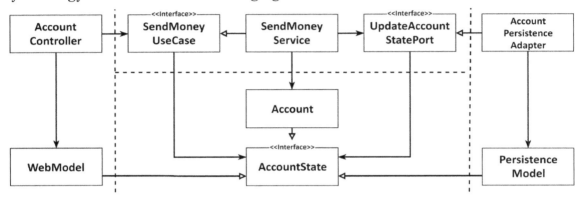

Figure 8.4: With the domain model and the adapter models implementing the same "state" interface, each layer only needs to map objects it receives from other layers – one way

In this strategy, the models in all layers implement the same interface, which encapsulates the state of the domain model by providing getter methods for the relevant attributes.

The domain model itself can implement a rich behavior, which we can access from our services within the application layer. If we want to pass a domain object to the outer layers, we can do so without mapping, since the domain object implements the state interface expected by the incoming and outgoing ports.

The outer layers can then decide whether they can work with the interface or whether they need to map it into their own model. They cannot inadvertently modify the state of the domain object since the modifying behavior is not exposed by the state interface.

Objects we pass from an outer layer into the application layer also implement this state interface. The application layer then has to map it into the real domain model in order to get access to its behavior. This mapping plays well with the DDD concept of a factory. A factory in terms of DDD is responsible for reconstituting a domain object from a certain state, which is exactly what we are doing (*Domain-Driven Design by Eric Evans, Addison-Wesley, 2004, p. 158*)

The mapping responsibility is clear: if a layer receives an object from another layer, we map it into something the layer can work with. Thus, each layer only maps one way, making this the "one-way" mapping strategy.

With the mapping distributed across layers, however, this strategy is conceptually more difficult than the other strategies.

This strategy plays out its strength best if the models across the layers are similar. For read-only operations, for instance, the web layer might not need to map into its own model at all, since the state interface provides all the information it needs.

When to Use Which Mapping Strategy?

This is the million-dollar question, isn't it?

The answer is the usual, dissatisfying, "It depends."

Since each mapping strategy has different advantages and disadvantages, we should resist the urge to define a single strategy as a hard-and-fast global rule for the whole codebase. This goes against our instincts, as it feels untidy to mix patterns within the same code base. But knowingly choosing a pattern that is not the best pattern for a certain job, just to serve our sense of tidiness, is irresponsible, plain and simple.

Also, as software evolves over time, the strategy that was the best for the job yesterday might not still be the best for the job today. Instead of starting with a fixed mapping strategy and keeping it over time – no matter what – we might start with a simple strategy that allows us to quickly evolve the code and later move to a more complex one that helps us to better decouple the layers.

In order to decide which strategy to use and when we need to agree upon a set of guidelines within the team. These guidelines should answer the question of which mapping strategy should be the first choice in which situation. They should also answer *why* they are the first choice so that we are able to evaluate whether those reasons still apply after some time.

We might, for example, define different mapping guidelines for modifying use cases than we do for queries. Also, we might want to use different mapping strategies between the web and application layers and between the application and persistence layers.

Guidelines for these situations might look like this:

If we are working on a *modifying use case*, the "full mapping" strategy is the first choice *between the web and application layers*, in order to decouple the use cases from one another. This gives us clear per-use-case validation rules and we won't have to deal with fields we don't need in a certain use case.

If we are working on a *modifying use case*, the "no mapping" strategy is the first choice *between the application and persistence layers* in order to be able to quickly evolve the code without mapping overhead. As soon as we have to deal with persistence issues in the application layer, however, we move to a "two-way" mapping strategy to keep persistence issues in the persistence layer.

If we are working on a *query*, the "no mapping" strategy is the first choice *between the web and application layers* and *between the application and persistence layers* in order to be able to quickly evolve the code without mapping overhead. As soon as we have to deal with web or persistence issues in the application layer, however, we move to a "two-way" mapping strategy between the web and application layers or the application layer and the persistence layer, respectively.

In order to successfully apply guidelines like these, they must be present in the minds of developers. So, the guidelines should be discussed and revised continuously as a team effort.

How Does This Help Me Build Maintainable Software?

With incoming and outgoing ports acting as gatekeepers between the layers of our application, they define how the layers communicate with each other and thus whether and how we map between layers.

With narrow ports in place for each use case, we can choose different mapping strategies for different use cases, and even evolve them over time without affecting other use cases, thus selecting the best strategy for a certain situation at a certain time.

This selection of mapping strategies per situation certainly is harder and requires more communication than simply using the same mapping strategy for all situations, but it will reward the team with a codebase that does just what it needs to do and is easier to maintain, as long as the mapping guidelines are known.

Assembling the Application

Now that we have implemented some use cases, web adapters, and persistence adapters, we need to assemble them into a working application. As discussed in *Chapter 3, Organizing Code*, we rely on a dependency injection mechanism to instantiate our classes and wire them together at startup. In this chapter, we will discuss some approaches for how we can do this with plain Java and the Spring and Spring Boot frameworks.

Why Even Care about Assembly?

Why aren't we just instantiating the use cases and adapters when and where we need them? Because we want to keep the code dependencies pointing in the right direction. Remember: all dependencies should point inward, toward the domain code of our application, so that the domain code doesn't have to change when something in the outer layers changes.

If a use case needs to call a persistence adapter and just instantiates it itself, we have created a code dependency in the wrong direction. This is why we created outgoing port interfaces. The use case only knows an interface and is provided an implementation of this interface at runtime.

A nice side effect of this programming style is that the code we are creating is much better testable. If we can pass all the objects a class needs into its constructor, we can choose to pass in mocks instead of the real objects, which makes it easy to create an isolated unit test for the class.

So, who's responsible for creating our object instances? And how do we do it without violating the dependency rule?

The answer is that there must be a configuration component that is neutral to our architecture and that has a dependency to *all* classes in order to instantiate them, as shown in the following figure:

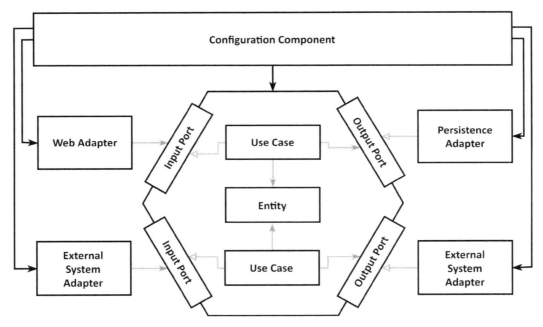

Figure 9.1: A neutral configuration component may access all classes in order to instantiate them

In the clean architecture introduced in *Chapter 2, Inverting Dependencies*, this configuration component would be in the outermost circle, which may access all inner layers, as defined by the dependency rule.

The configuration component is responsible for assembling a working application from the parts we provided. It must:

- Create web adapter instances
- Ensure that HTTP requests are actually routed to the web adapters
- Create use case instances
- Provide web adapters with use case instances
- Create persistence adapter instances
- Provide use cases with persistence adapter instances
- Ensure that the persistence adapters can actually access the database

Besides that, the configuration component should be able to access certain sources of configuration parameters, such as configuration files or command-line parameters. During application assembly, the configuration component then passes these parameters on to the application components to control behavior, such as which database to access or which server to use for sending an email.

These are a lot of responsibilities (read: "reasons to change"). Aren't we violating the Single Responsibility Principle here? Yes, we are, but if we want to keep the rest of the application clean, we need an outside component that takes care of the wiring. And this component has to know all the moving parts to assemble them into a working application.

Assembling via Plain Code

There are several ways to implement a configuration component responsible for assembling the application. If we are building an application without the support of a dependency injection framework, we can create such a component with plain code:

```
package copyeditor.configuration;


class Application {


  public static void main(String[] args) {


    AccountRepository accountRepository = new AccountRepository();
```

```
ActivityRepository activityRepository = new ActivityRepository();
AccountPersistenceAdapter accountPersistenceAdapter =
    new AccountPersistenceAdapter(accountRepository, activityRepository);


SendMoneyUseCase sendMoneyUseCase =
    new SendMoneyUseService(
        accountPersistenceAdapter,  // LoadAccountPort
        accountPersistenceAdapter); // UpdateAccountStatePort


SendMoneyController sendMoneyController =
    new SendMoneyController(sendMoneyUseCase);


startProcessingWebRequests(sendMoneyController);


    }
}
```

This code snippet is a simplified example of how such a configuration component might look. In Java, an application is started from the **main** method. Within this method, we instantiate all the classes we need, from the web controller to the persistence adapter, and wire them together.

Finally, we call the mystic method named **startProcessingWebRequests()**, which exposes the web controller via HTTP. This method is just a placeholder for any bootstrapping logic that is necessary to expose our web adapters via HTTP (we don't really want to implement this ourselves). The application is then ready to process requests.

This plain code approach is the most basic way of assembling an application. It has some drawbacks, however.

First of all, the preceding code is for an application that has only a single web controller, use case, and persistence adapter. Imagine how much code like this we would have to produce to bootstrap a full-blown enterprise application.

Second, since we are instantiating all classes ourselves from outside of their packages, those classes all need to be public. This means, for example, that Java doesn't prevent a use case directly accessing a persistence adapter since it's public. It would be nice if we could avoid unwanted dependencies like this by using package-private visibility.

Luckily, there are dependency injection frameworks that can do the dirty work for us while still maintaining package-private dependencies. The Spring Framework is currently the most popular one in the Java world. Spring also provides web and database support, among a lot of other things, so we don't have to implement the mystic **startProcessingWebRequests()** method after all.

Assembling via Spring's Classpath Scanning

If we use the Spring Framework to assemble our application, the result is called the application context. The application context contains all objects that together make up the application ("beans" in Java lingo).

Spring offers several approaches to assemble an application context, each having its own advantages and drawbacks. Let's start by discussing the most popular (and most convenient) approach: classpath scanning.

With classpath scanning, Spring goes through all the classes that are available in the classpath and searches for classes that are annotated with the **@Component** annotation. The framework then creates an object from each of these classes. The classes should have a constructor that takes all required fields as an argument, like our **AccountPersistenceAdapter** from *Chapter 6, Implementing a Persistence Adapter*:

```
@RequiredArgsConstructor
@Component
class AccountPersistenceAdapter implements
    LoadAccountPort,
    UpdateAccountStatePort {


  private final AccountRepository accountRepository;
  private final ActivityRepository activityRepository;
  private final AccountMapper accountMapper;


  @Override
  public Account loadAccount(
        AccountId accountId,
        LocalDateTime baselineDate) {
    // ...
  }
```

```
@Override
public void updateActivities(Account account) {
  // ...
}


}
```

In this case, we didn't even write the constructor ourselves but instead let the Lombok library do it for us using the **@RequiredArgsConstructor** annotation, which creates a constructor that takes all **final** fields as arguments.

Spring will find this constructor and search for **@Component**-annotated classes of the required argument types and instantiate them in a similar manner to add them to the application context. Once all the required objects are available, it will finally call the constructor of **AccountPersistenceAdapter** and add the resulting object to the application context as well.

Classpath scanning is a very convenient way of assembling an application. We only have to sprinkle some **@Component** annotations across the code base and provide the right constructors.

We can also create our own stereotype annotation for Spring to pick up. We could, for example, create a **@PersistenceAdapter** annotation:

```
@Target({ElementType.TYPE})

@Retention(RetentionPolicy.RUNTIME)

@Documented

@Component

public @interface PersistenceAdapter {


  @AliasFor(annotation = Component.class)
  String value() default "";


}
```

This annotation is meta-annotated with **@Component** to let Spring know that it should be picked up during classpath scanning. We could now use **@PersistenceAdapter** instead of **@Component** to mark our persistence adapter classes as parts of our application. With this annotation, we have made our architecture more evident to people reading the code.

The classpath scanning approach has its drawbacks, however. First, it's invasive in that it requires us to put a framework-specific annotation in our classes. If you are a clean architecture hardliner, you'd say that this is forbidden as it binds our code to a specific framework.

I'd say that in usual application development, a single annotation on a class is not such a big deal and can easily be refactored, if at all necessary.

In other contexts, however, such as when building a library or a framework for other developers to use, this might be a no-go, since we don't want to encumber our users with a dependency on the Spring Framework.

Another potential drawback of the classpath scanning approach is that magic things might happen. And by "magic" I mean the bad kind of magic, causing inexplicable effects that might take days to figure out if you are not a Spring expert.

Magic happens because classpath scanning is a very blunt weapon to use for application assembly. We simply point Spring at the parent package of our application and tell it to go looking for **@Component**-annotated classes within this package.

Do you know by heart every single class that exists within your application? Probably not. There's bound to be a class that we don't actually want to have in the application context. Perhaps this class even manipulates the application context in evil ways, causing errors that are hard to track.

Let's look at an alternative approach that gives us a little more control.

Assembling via Spring's Java Config

While classpath scanning is the cudgel of application assembly, Spring's Java Config is the scalpel. This approach is similar to the plain code approach introduced earlier in this chapter, but it's less messy and provides us with a framework so that we don't have to code everything by hand.

In this approach, we create configuration classes, each responsible for constructing a set of beans that are to be added to the application context.

For example, we could create a configuration class that is responsible for instantiating all of our persistence adapters:

```
@Configuration
@EnableJpaRepositories
class PersistenceAdapterConfiguration {
```

```
@Bean
AccountPersistenceAdapter accountPersistenceAdapter(
        AccountRepository accountRepository,
        ActivityRepository activityRepository,
        AccountMapper accountMapper){
    return new AccountPersistenceAdapter(
      accountRepository,
      activityRepository,
      accountMapper);
}

@Bean
AccountMapper accountMapper(){
    return new AccountMapper();
}


  }
```

The **@Configuration** annotation marks this class as a configuration class to be picked up by Spring's classpath scanning. So, in this case, we are still using classpath scanning, but we only pick up our configuration classes instead of every single bean, which reduces the chance of evil magic happening.

The beans themselves are created within the **@Bean**-annotated factory methods of our configuration classes. In the preceding case, we add a persistence adapter to the application context. It needs two repositories and a mapper as input to its constructor. Spring automatically provides these objects as input to the factory methods.

But where does Spring get the repository objects from? If they are created manually in a factory method of another configuration class, then Spring would automatically provide them as parameters to the factory methods of the preceding code example. In this case, however, they are created by Spring itself, triggered by the **@EnableJpaRepositories** annotation. If Spring Boot finds this annotation, it will automatically provide implementations for all of the Spring Data repository interfaces we have defined.

If you are familiar with Spring Boot, you might know that we could have added the `@EnableJpaRepositories` annotation to the main application class instead of our custom configuration class. Yes, this is possible, but it would activate Java Persistence API (JPA) repositories every time the application is started up – even if we start the application within a test that doesn't actually need persistence. So, by moving such "feature annotations" to a separate configuration "module," we have just become much more flexible and can start up parts of our application instead of always having to start the whole thing.

With the `PersistenceAdapterConfiguration` class, we have created a tightly scoped persistence module that instantiates all the objects we need in our persistence layer. It will be automatically picked up by Spring's classpath scanning and we will still have full control over which beans are actually added to the application context.

Similarly, we could create configuration classes for web adapters, or for certain modules within our application layer. We could then create an application context that contains certain modules but mocks the beans of other modules, which gives us great flexibility in tests. We could even push the code of each of those modules into its own codebase, its own package, or its own Java Archive (JAR) file without much refactoring.

Also, this approach does not force us to sprinkle `@Component` annotations all over our codebase, as the classpath scanning approach does. So, we can keep our application layer clean without any dependency on the Spring Framework (or any other framework, for that matter).

There is a catch with this solution, however. If the configuration class is not within the same package as the classes of the beans it creates (the persistence adapter classes in this case), those classes must be public. To restrict visibility, we can use packages as module boundaries and create a dedicated configuration class within each package. This way, we cannot use sub-packages, though, as will be discussed in *Chapter 10, Enforcing Architecture Boundaries*.

How Does This Help Me Build Maintainable Software?

Spring and Spring Boot (and similar frameworks) provide a lot of features that make our lives easier. One of the main features is assembling applications out of the parts (classes) that we, as application developers, provide.

Classpath scanning is a very convenient feature. We only have to point Spring to a package and it assembles an application from the classes it finds. This allows for rapid development, with us not having to think about the application as a whole.

Once the code base grows, however, this quickly leads to a lack of transparency. We don't know which beans exactly are loaded into the application context. Also, we cannot easily startup isolated parts of the application context to use in tests.

By creating a dedicated configuration component responsible for assembling our application, we can liberate our application code from this responsibility (read: "reason for change" – remember the "S" in "SOLID"?). We are rewarded with highly cohesive modules that we can start up in isolation from each other and that we can easily move around within our codebase. As usual, this comes at the price of spending some extra time on maintaining this configuration component.

10
Enforcing Architecture Boundaries

We have talked a lot about architecture in the previous chapters and it feels good to have a target architecture to guide us in our decisions on how to craft code and where to put it.

In every above-playsize software project, however, architecture tends to erode over time. Boundaries between layers weaken, code becomes harder to test, and we generally need more and more time to implement new features.

In this chapter, we will discuss some measures that we can take to enforce the boundaries within our architecture and thus fight architecture erosion.

Boundaries and Dependencies

Before we talk about different ways of enforcing architecture boundaries, let's discuss where the boundaries lie within our architecture and what "enforcing a boundary" actually means:

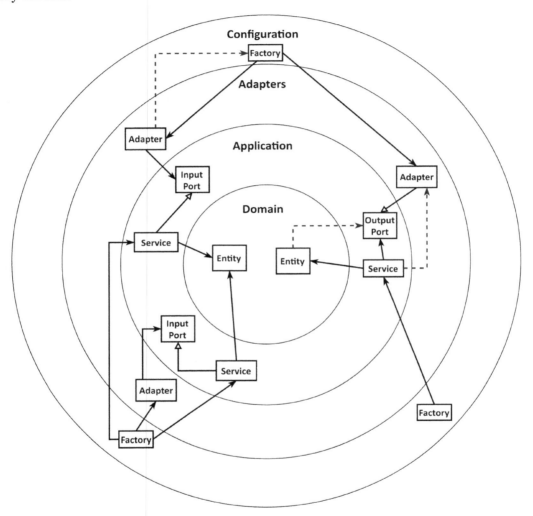

Figure 10.1: Enforcing architecture boundaries means enforcing that dependencies point in the right direction. Dashed arrows mark dependencies that are not allowed according to our architecture

The preceding figure shows how the elements of our hexagonal architecture might be distributed across four layers resembling the generic clean architecture approach introduced in *Chapter 2, Inverting Dependencies*.

The innermost layer contains domain entities. The application layer may access those domain entities to implement use cases within application services. Adapters access those services through incoming ports or are being accessed by those services through outgoing ports. Finally, the configuration layer contains factories that create adapter and service objects and provides them to a dependency injection mechanism.

In the preceding figure, our architecture boundaries become pretty clear. There is a boundary between each layer and its next inward and outward neighbors. According to the dependency rule, dependencies that cross such layer boundaries must always point inward.

This chapter is about ways to enforce the dependency rule. We want to make sure that there are no illegal dependencies that point in the wrong direction (dashed arrows in the figure).

Visibility Modifiers

Let's start with the most basic tool that Java provides us for enforcing boundaries: visibility modifiers.

Visibility modifiers have been a topic in almost every entry-level job interview I have conducted in the last couple of years. I would ask the interviewee what visibility modifiers Java provides and what their differences are.

Most of the interviewees only list the public, protected, and private modifiers. Almost none know the package-private (or "default") modifier. This is always a welcome opportunity for me to ask some questions about why such a visibility modifier would make sense in order to find out whether the interviewee could abstract the answer from their previous knowledge.

So, why is the package-private modifier such an important modifier? Because it allows us to use Java packages to group classes into cohesive "modules." Classes within such a module can access each other but cannot be accessed from outside of the package. We can then choose to make specific classes public to act as entry points to the module. This reduces the risk of accidentally violating the dependency rule by introducing a dependency that points in the wrong direction.

Let's have another look at the package structure discussed in *Chapter 3, Organizing Code*, with visibility modifiers in mind:

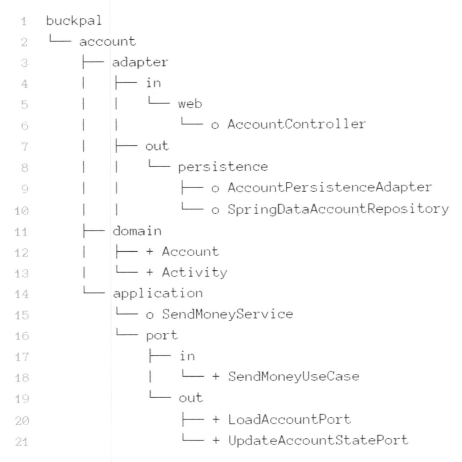

```
1  buckpal
2  └── account
3      ├── adapter
4      │   ├── in
5      │   │   └── web
6      │   │       └── o AccountController
7      │   ├── out
8      │   │   └── persistence
9      │   │       ├── o AccountPersistenceAdapter
10     │   │       └── o SpringDataAccountRepository
11     ├── domain
12     │   ├── + Account
13     │   └── + Activity
14     └── application
15         └── o SendMoneyService
16         └── port
17             ├── in
18             │   └── + SendMoneyUseCase
19             └── out
20                 ├── + LoadAccountPort
21                 └── + UpdateAccountStatePort
```

Figure 10.2: Package structure with visibility modifiers.

We can make the classes in the **persistence** package package-private (marked with "o" in the preceding tree) because they don't need to be accessed by the outside world. The persistence adapter is accessed through the output ports it implements. For the same reason, we can make the **SendMoneyService** class package-private. Dependency injection mechanisms usually use reflection to instantiate classes, so they will still be able to instantiate those classes even if they are package-private.

With Spring, this approach only works if we use the classpath scanning approach discussed in *Chapter 9, Assembling the Application*, however, since the other approaches require us to create instances of those objects ourselves, which requires public access.

The rest of the classes in the example have to be public (marked with "+") by definition of the architecture: the **domain** package needs to be accessible by the other layers and the **application** layer needs to be accessible by the **web** and **persistence** adapters.

The package-private modifier is awesome for small modules with no more than a handful of classes. Once a package reaches a certain number of classes, however, it grows confusing to have so many classes in the same package. In this case, I like to create sub-packages to make the code easier to find (and, I admit, to satisfy my need for aesthetics). This is where the package-private modifier fails to deliver since Java treats sub-packages as different packages and we cannot access a package-private member of a sub-package. So, members in sub-packages must be public, exposing them to the outside world and thus making our architecture vulnerable to illegal dependencies.

Post-Compile Checks

As soon as we use the public modifier on a class, the compiler will let any other class use it, even if the direction of the dependency points in the wrong direction according to our architecture. Since the compiler won't help us out in these cases, we have to find other means to check that the dependency rule isn't violated.

One way is to introduce post-compile checks – that is, checks that are conducted at runtime when the code has already been compiled. Such runtime checks are best run during automated tests within a continuous integration build.

A tool that supports this kind of check for Java is ArchUnit (https://github.com/TNG/ArchUnit). Among other things, ArchUnit provides an API to check whether dependencies point in the expected direction. If it finds a violation, it will throw an exception. It's best run from within a test based on a unit testing framework such as JUnit, making the test fail in the event of a dependency violation.

With ArchUnit, we can now check the dependencies between our layers, assuming that each layer has its own package, as defined in the package structure discussed in the previous section. For example, we can check that there is no dependency from the domain layer to the outward-lying application layer:

```
class DependencyRuleTests {

    @Test
    void domainLayerDoesNotDependOnApplicationLayer() {
        noClasses()
            .that()
            .resideInAPackage("buckpal.domain..")
            .should()
```

```
          .dependOnClassesThat()
          .resideInAnyPackage("buckpal.application..")
          .check(new ClassFileImporter()
              .importPackages("buckpal.."));

    }


}
```

With a little work, we can even create a kind of domain-specific language (DSL) on top of the ArchUnit API that allows us to specify all relevant packages within our hexagonal architecture and then automatically checks whether all the dependencies between those packages point in the right direction:

```
class DependencyRuleTests {


  @Test
  void validateRegistrationContextArchitecture() {
    HexagonalArchitecture.boundedContext("account")
        .withDomainLayer("domain")
        .withAdaptersLayer("adapter")
          .incoming("web")
          .outgoing("persistence")
          .and()
        .withApplicationLayer("application")
          .services("service")
          .incomingPorts("port.in")
          .outgoingPorts("port.out")
          .and()
        .withConfiguration("configuration")
        .check(new ClassFileImporter()
            .importPackages("buckpal.."));

    }


}
```

In the preceding code example, we first specify the parent package of our bounded context (which might also be a complete application if it spans only a single bounded context). We then go on to specify the sub-packages for the domain, adapter, application, and configuration layers. The final call to `check()` will then execute a set of checks, verifying that the package dependencies are valid according to the dependency rule. The code for this hexagonal architecture DSL is available in the `HexagonalArchitecture` class of the example project at https://github.com/thombergs/buckpal.

While post-compile checks can be a great help in fighting illegal dependencies, they are not fail-safe. If we misspell the package name `buckpal` in the preceding code example, for instance, the test will find no classes and thus no dependency violations. A single typo or, more importantly, a single refactoring renaming a package can make the whole test useless. We might fix this by adding a check that fails if no classes are found, but it's still vulnerable to refactorings. Post-compile checks always have to be maintained parallel to the codebase.

Build Artifacts

Until now, our only tool for demarcating architecture boundaries within our codebase has been packaged. All of our code has been part of the same monolithic build artifact.

A build artifact is the result of a (hopefully automated) build process. Currently, the most popular build tools in the Java world are Maven and Gradle. So, until now, imagine we had a single Maven or Gradle build script and we could call Maven or Gradle to compile, test, and package the code of our application into a single JAR file.

One main feature of build tools is dependency resolution. To transform a certain codebase into a build artifact, a build tool first checks whether all the artifacts that the code base depends on are available. If not, it tries to load them from an artifact repository. If this fails, the build will fail with an error, before even trying to compile the code.

We can leverage this to enforce the dependencies (and thus, enforce the boundaries) between the modules and layers of our architecture. For each such module or layer, we create a separate build module with its own codebase and its own build artifact (JAR file) as a result. In the build script of each module, we specify only those dependencies to other modules that are allowed according to our architecture. Developers can no longer inadvertently create illegal dependencies because the classes are not even available on the classpath and they would run into compile errors:

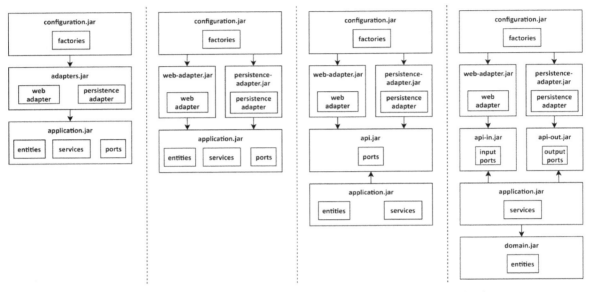

Figure 10.3: Different ways of dividing our architecture into multiple
build artifacts to prohibit illegal dependencies

The preceding figure shows an incomplete set of options to divide our architecture into separate build artifacts.

Starting on the left, we see a basic three-module build with a separate build artifact for the configuration, adapter, and application layers. The configuration module may access the adapters module, which in turn may access the application module. The configuration module may also access the application module due to the implicit, transitive dependency between them.

Note that the adapter's module contains the web adapter as well as the persistence adapter. This means that the build tool will not prohibit dependencies between those adapters. While dependencies between those adapters are not strictly forbidden by the dependency rule (since both adapters are within the same outer layer), in most cases it's sensible to keep adapters isolated from each other.

After all, we usually don't want changes in the persistence layer to leak into the web layer and vice versa (remember the Single Responsibility Principle).

The same holds true for other types of adapters, such as adapters connecting our application to a certain third-party API. We don't want details of that API leaking into other adapters by adding accidental dependencies between adapters.

Thus, we may split the single adapters module into multiple build modules, one for each adapter, as shown in the second column of *Figure 10.2*.

Next, we could decide to split up the application module further. It currently contains the incoming and outgoing ports to our application, the services that implement or use those ports, and the domain entities that should contain much of our domain logic.

If we decide that our domain entities are not to be used as transfer objects within our ports (that is, we want to disallow the "No Mapping" strategy from *Chapter 8, Mapping between Boundaries*), we can apply the Dependency Inversion Principle and pull out a separate API module that contains only the port interfaces (the third column in *Figure 10.2*).

The adapter modules and the application module may access the API module, but not the other way around. The API module does not have access to the domain entities and cannot use them within the port interfaces. Also, the adapters no longer have direct access to the entities and services, so they must go through the ports.

We can even go a step further and split the API module in two, one part containing only the incoming ports and the other part only containing the outgoing ports (the fourth column in *Figure 10.1*). This way, we can make very clear whether a certain adapter is an incoming adapter or an outgoing adapter by declaring a dependency only to the input or the outgoing ports.

Also, we could split the application module even further, creating a module containing only the services and another containing only the domain entities. This ensures that the entities don't access the services and it would allow other applications (with different use cases and thus different services) to use the same domain entities by simply declaring a dependency on the domain build artifact.

Figure 10.2 illustrates that there are a lot of different ways to divide an application into build modules, and there are of course more than just the four ways depicted in the figure. The gist is that the finer we cut our modules, the stronger we can control dependencies between them. The finer we cut, however, the more mapping we have to do between those modules, enforcing one of the mapping strategies introduced in *Chapter 8, Mapping between Boundaries*.

Besides that, demarcating architecture boundaries with build modules has a number of advantages over using simple packages as boundaries.

First, build tools absolutely hate circular dependencies. Circular dependencies are bad because a change in one module within the circle would potentially mean a change in all other modules within the circle, which is a violation of the single responsibility principle. Build tools don't allow circular dependencies because they would run into an endless loop while trying to resolve them. Thus, we can be sure that there are no circular dependencies between our build modules.

The Java compiler, on the other hand, doesn't care at all whether there is a circular dependency between two or more packages.

Second, build modules allow isolated code changes within certain modules without having to take the other modules into consideration. Imagine we have to do a major refactoring in the application layer that causes temporary compile errors in a certain adapter. If the adapters and application layer are within the same build module, most IDEs will insist that all compile errors in the adapters must be fixed before we can run the tests in the application layer, even though the tests don't need the adapters to compile. If the application layer is in its own build module, however, the IDE won't care about the adapters at that time, and we could run the application layer tests at will. The same goes for running a build process with Maven or Gradle: if both layers were in the same build module, the build would fail due to compile errors in either layer.

So, multiple build modules allow isolated changes in each module. We could even choose to put each module into its own code repository, allowing different teams to maintain different modules.

Finally, with each inter-module dependency explicitly declared in a build script, adding a new dependency becomes a conscious act instead of an accident. A developer who needs access to a certain class they currently cannot access will hopefully give some thought to the question of whether the dependency is really reasonable before adding it to the build script.

These advantages come with the added cost of having to maintain a build script, though, so the architecture should be somewhat stable before splitting it into different build modules.

How Does This Help Me Build Maintainable Software?

Software architecture is basically all about managing dependencies between architecture elements. If the dependencies become a big ball of mud, the architecture becomes a big ball of mud.

So, to preserve the architecture over time, we need to continually make sure that dependencies point in the right direction.

When producing new code or refactoring existing code, we should keep the package structure in mind and use package-private visibility when possible to avoid dependencies on classes that should not be accessed from outside the package.

If we need to enforce architecture boundaries within a single build module, and the package-private modifier doesn't work because the package structure won't allow it, we can make use of post-compile tools such as ArchUnit.

And anytime we feel that the architecture is stable enough, we should extract architecture elements into their own build modules because this gives explicit control over the dependencies.

All three approaches can be combined to enforce architecture boundaries and thus keep the code base maintainable over time.

11

Taking Shortcuts Consciously

In the preface of this book, I cursed the fact that we feel forced to take shortcuts all the time, building up a great heap of technical debt we never have the chance to pay back.

To prevent shortcuts, we must be able to identify them. So, the goal of this chapter is to raise awareness of some potential shortcuts and discuss their effects.

With this information, we can identify and fix accidental shortcuts. Or, if justified, we can even consciously opt-in to the effects of a shortcut.

Imagine the preceding sentence in a book about construction engineering or, even scarier, in a book about avionics. Most of us, however, are not building the software equivalent of a skyscraper or an airplane. And software is soft and can be changed more easily than hardware, so sometimes it's actually more economical to (consciously) take a shortcut first and fix it later (or never).

Why Shortcuts Are Like Broken Windows

In 1969, psychologist Philip Zimbardo conducted an experiment to test a theory that later became known as the Broken Windows Theory (https://www.theatlantic.com/ideastour/archive/windows.html).

He parked one car without license plates in a Bronx neighborhood and another in an allegedly "better" neighborhood in Palo Alto. Then he waited.

The car in the Bronx was picked clean of valuable parts within 24 hours and then passersby started to randomly destroy it.

The car in Palo Alto was not touched for a week, so Zimbardo smashed a window. From then on, the car had a similar fate to the car in the Bronx and was destroyed in the same short amount of time by people walking by.

The people taking part in looting and destroying the cars came from all social classes and included people who were otherwise law-abiding and well-behaved citizens.

This human behavior has become known as the Broken Windows Theory. In my own words:

> As soon as something looks run-down, damaged, [insert negative adjective here], or generally untended, the human brain feels that it's OK to make it more run-down, damaged, or [insert negative adjective here].

This theory applies to many areas of life:

- In a neighborhood where vandalism is common, the threshold to loot or damage an untended car is low.

- When a car has a broken window, the threshold to damage it further is low, even in a "good" neighborhood.

- In an untidy bedroom, the threshold to throw our clothes on the ground instead of putting them into the wardrobe is low.

- In a group of people where bullying is common, the threshold to bully just a little more is low.

Applied to working with code, this means:

- When working on a low-quality code base, the threshold to add more low-quality code is low.

- When working on a codebase with a lot of coding violations, the threshold to add another coding violation is low.

- When working on a codebase with a lot of shortcuts, the threshold to add another shortcut is low.

With all this in mind, is it really a surprise that the quality of many so-called "legacy" codebases has eroded so badly over time?

The Responsibility of Starting Clean

While working with code doesn't really feel like looting a car, we all are unconsciously subject to Broken Windows psychology. This makes it important to start a project clean, with as few shortcuts and as little technical debt as possible. Because, as soon as a shortcut creeps in, it acts as a broken window and attracts more shortcuts.

Since software projects are often very expensive and long-running endeavors, keeping broken windows at bay is a huge responsibility for us as software developers. We may even not be the ones finishing the project and others have to take over. For them, it's a legacy codebase they don't have a connection to, lowering the threshold for creating broken windows even further.

There are times, however, when we decide that a shortcut is a pragmatic thing to do, be it because the part of the code we are working on is not that important to the project as a whole, or that we are prototyping, or for economical reasons.

We should take great care to document such consciously added shortcuts, perhaps in the form of Architecture Decision Records (ADRs) as proposed by Michael Nygard in his blog (http://thinkrelevance.com/blog/2011/11/15/documenting-architecture-decisions). We owe that to our future selves and to our successors. If every member of the team is aware of this documentation, it will even reduce the Broken Windows effect, because the team will know that the shortcuts have been taken consciously and for good reason.

The following sections each discuss a pattern that can be considered a shortcut in the hexagonal architecture style presented in this book. We will have a look at the effects of the shortcuts and the arguments that speak for and against taking them.

Sharing Models between Use Cases

In *Chapter 4, Implementing a Use Case*, I argued that different use cases should have a different input and output model, meaning that the types of input parameters and the types of return values should be different.

The following figure shows an example where two use cases share the same input model:

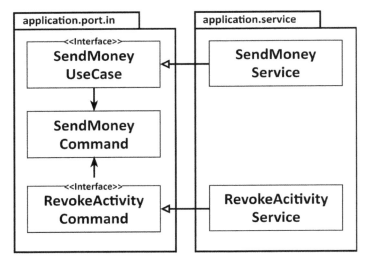

Figure 11.1: Sharing the input or output model between use cases leads to coupling between the use cases

The effect of sharing, in this case, is that **SendMoneyUseCase** and **RevokeActivityUseCase** are coupled to each other. If we change something within the shared **SendMoneyCommand** class, both use cases are affected. They share a reason to change in terms of the single responsibility principle. The same is true if both use cases share the same output model.

Sharing input and output models between use cases is valid if the use cases are functionally bound – that is, if they share a certain requirement. In this case, *we actually want both use cases to be affected if we change a certain detail.*

If both use cases should be able to evolve separately from each other, however, this is a shortcut. In this case, we should separate the use cases from the start, even if it means duplicating input and output classes if they look the same at the start.

So, when building multiple use cases around a similar concept, it's worthwhile to regularly ask the question of whether use cases should evolve separately from each other. As soon as the answer becomes a "yes," it's time to separate the input and output models.

Using Domain Entities as Input or Output Models

If we have an **Account** domain entity and an incoming port, **SendMoneyUseCase**, we might be tempted to use the entity as the input and/or output model of the incoming port, as shown in the following figure:

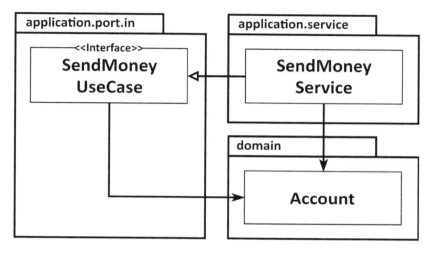

Figure 11.2: Using a domain entity as the input or output model of a use case couples the domain entity to the use case

The incoming port has a dependency on the domain entity. The consequence of this is that we have added another reason for the **Account** entity to change.

Wait, the **Account** entity doesn't have a dependency on the **SendMoneyUseCase** incoming port (it's the other way around), so how can the incoming port be a reason to change for the entity?

Say we need some information about an account in the use case that is not currently available in the **Account** entity. This information is ultimately not to be stored in the **Account** entity, however, but in a different domain or bounded context. We are tempted to add a new field to the **Account** entity nevertheless because it's already available in the use case interface.

For simple create or update use cases, a domain entity in the use case interface may be fine. Since the entity contains exactly the information, we need to persist its state in the database.

As soon as a use case is not simply about updating a couple of fields in the database, but instead implements more complex domain logic (potentially delegating part of the domain logic to a rich domain entity), we should use a dedicated input and output model for the use case interface, because we don't want changes in the use case to propagate to the domain entity.

What makes this shortcut dangerous is the fact that many use cases start their lives as a simple create or update use case only to become beasts of complex domain logic over time. This is especially true in an agile environment where we start with a minimum viable product and add complexity on the way forward. So, if we used a domain entity as the input model at the start, we must find the point in time to replace it with a dedicated input model that is independent of the domain entity.

Skipping Incoming Ports

While the outgoing ports are necessary to invert the dependency between the application layer and the outgoing adapters (to make the dependencies point inward), we don't need the incoming ports for dependency inversion. We could decide to let the incoming adapters access our application services directly, without incoming ports in between, as shown in the following figure:

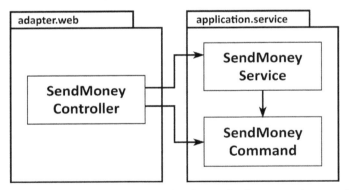

Figure 11.3: Without incoming ports, we lose clearly marked entry points to the domain logic

By removing the incoming ports, we have reduced a layer of abstraction between incoming adapters and the application layer. Removing layers of abstraction usually feels rather good.

The incoming ports, however, define the entry points into our application core. Once we remove them, we must know more about the internals of our application to find out which service method we can call to implement a certain use case. By maintaining dedicated incoming ports, we can identify the entry points to the application at a glance. This makes it especially easy for new developers to get their bearings in the codebase.

Another reason to keep the incoming ports is that they allow us to easily enforce architecture. With the enforcement options from *Chapter 10, Enforcing Architecture Boundaries*, we can make certain that incoming adapters only call incoming ports and not application services. This makes every entry point into the application layer a very conscious decision. We can no longer accidentally call a service method that was not meant to be called from an incoming adapter.

If an application is small enough or only has a single incoming adapter so that we can grasp the whole control flow without the help of incoming ports, we might want to do without incoming ports. However, how often can we say that we know that an application will stay small or will only ever have a single incoming adapter over its whole lifetime?

Skipping Application Services

Aside from the incoming ports, for certain use cases, we might want to skip the application layer as a whole, as shown in the following figure:

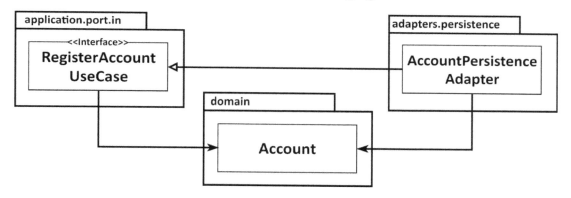

Figure 11.4: Without application services, we don't have a specified location for domain logic

Here, the `AccountPersistenceAdapter` class within an outgoing adapter directly implements an incoming port and replaces the application service that usually implements an incoming port.

It is very tempting to do this for simple CRUD use cases, since in this case an application service usually only forwards a create, update, or delete request to the persistence adapter, without adding any domain logic. Instead of forwarding, we can let the persistence adapter implement the use case directly.

This, however, requires a shared model between the incoming adapter and the outgoing adapter, which is the **Account** domain entity in this case, so it usually means that we are using the domain model as the input model as described previously.

Furthermore, we no longer have a representation of the use case within our application core. If a CRUD use case grows to something more complex over time, it's tempting to add domain logic directly to the outgoing adapter, since the use case has already been implemented there. This decentralizes the domain logic, making it harder to find and to maintain.

In the end, to prevent boilerplate pass-through services, we might choose to skip the application services for simple CRUD use cases after all. Then, however, the team should develop clear guidelines to introduce an application service as soon as the use case is expected to do more than just create, update, or delete an entity.

How Does This Help Me Build Maintainable Software?

There are times when shortcuts make sense from an economic point of view. This chapter provided some insights into the consequences some shortcuts might have to help you decide whether to take them or not.

The discussion shows that it's tempting to introduce shortcuts for simple CRUD use cases, since for them, implementing the whole architecture feels like overkill (and the shortcuts don't feel like shortcuts). Since all applications start small, however, it's very important for the team to agree upon when a use case grows out of its CRUD state. Only then can the team replace the shortcuts with an architecture that is more maintainable in the long run.

Some use cases will never grow out of their CRUD state. For them, it might be more pragmatic to keep the shortcuts in place forever, as they don't really entail a maintenance overhead.

In any case, we should document the architecture and the decisions why we chose a certain shortcut so that we (or our successors) can re-evaluate the decisions in the future.

12
Deciding on an Architecture Style

So far, this book has presented an opinionated approach to building a web application in a hexagonal architecture style. From organizing code to taking shortcuts, we have answered many questions that this architecture style confronts us with.

Some of the answers in this book can be applied to the conventional layered architecture style. Some answers can only be implemented in a domain-centric approach such as the one proposed in this book. And some answers you might not even agree with, because they don't work in your experience.

The final questions we want answers for, however, are these: when should we actually use the hexagonal architecture style? And when should we instead stick with the conventional layered style (or any other style, for that matter)?

The Domain is King

It should have become obvious in the previous chapters that the main feature of a hexagonal architecture style is that we can develop the domain code free from diversions such as persistence concerns and dependencies upon external systems.

> *Evolving domain code free from external influence is the single most important argument for the hexagonal architecture style.*

This is why this architecture style is such a good match for Domain-Driven Design (DDD) practices. To state the obvious, in DDD the domain drives the development. And we can best reason about the domain if we don't have to think about persistence concerns and other technical aspects at the same time.

I would even go so far as to say that *domain-centric architecture styles such as the hexagonal style are enablers of DDD*. Without an architecture that puts the domain into the center of things, without inverting the dependencies toward the domain code, we have no chance of really doing DDD; the design will always be driven by other factors.

So, as a first indicator of whether to use the architecture style presented in this book or not, if the domain code is not the most important thing in your application, you probably don't need this architecture style.

Experience is Queen

We are creatures of habit. Habits automate decisions for us so we don't have to spend time on them. If there's a lion running toward us, we run. If we build a new web application, we use the layered architecture style. We have done it so often in the past that it has become a habit.

I'm not saying that this is necessarily a bad decision. Habits are just as good at helping us to make the right decision as they are at making a bad one. I'm saying that we are doing what we are experienced in. We are comfortable with what we have done in the past, so why should we change anything?

So, the only way to make an educated decision about an architecture style is by having experience in different architecture styles. If you are unsure about the hexagonal architecture style, try it out on a small module of the application that you are currently building. Get used to the concepts and get comfortable. Apply the ideas in this book, modify them, and add your own ideas to develop a style you are comfortable with.

This experience can then guide your next architecture decision.

It Depends

I would love to provide a list of multiple-choice questions to decide on an architecture style just like all those "Which Personality Type Are You?" and "What Kind of Dog Are You?" tests that regularly swirl around social media. I'm the "Defender" personality type and if I were a dog, I would apparently be a Pit bull.

But it isn't as easy as that. My answer to the question of which architecture style to choose remains the professional consultant's "It depends...". It depends on the type of software to be built. It depends on the role of the domain code. It depends on the experience of the team. And finally, it depends on being comfortable with a decision.

I hope, however, that this book has provided some sparks to help with the architecture question. If you have a story to tell about architecture decisions, with or without hexagonal architecture, I'd love to hear about it.

You can drop me an email at **tom@reflectoring.io**.

Index

About

All major keywords used in this book are captured alphabetically in this section. Each one is accompanied by the page number of where they appear.

A

adapter: 17, 23-28, 34-36, 44, 49-53, 55, 57, 59-61, 63-65, 67-69, 71-72, 80-84, 87-88, 93, 95-96, 102-106, 108-109, 115-116, 118-122, 131-132
anemic: 31, 44
annotation: 72, 82, 93, 105-109
application layer: 18, 25, 26, 27, 28, 36, 50, 52, 53, 57, 59, 92, 95, 96, 97, 98, 109, 115, 117, 120, 122, 130, 131
application service: 35, 43, 46, 50, 51, 59, 60, 72, 115, 130, 131, 132
ArchUnit: 117, 118, 123
architecture-code gap: 25
artifact: 119-121
assemble: 101, 103, 105
assembly: 101, 103, 107

B

behavior-driven: 80, 87
Broken Windows Theory: 4, 125, 126
bootstrap: 104
bounded context: 26, 64, 65, 119, 129
boundary: 22, 53, 77, 114, 115
broad service: 6, 8, 15, 35
brocken windows: 4, 125, 126, 127
builder: 40

business rule: 3, 14, 15, 16, 34, 35, 42, 43, 44, 45, 78

C

classpath: 105-109, 116, 120
clean architecture: 2, 11, 14, 15, 16, 17, 18, 23, 26, 62, 102, 107, 115
codebase: 8, 13, 18, 40, 47, 51, 62, 72, 88-89, 97-98, 109-110, 119-120, 126-127, 130
cohesive: 63, 110, 115
constructor: 16, 37, 39, 40, 71, 102, 105, 106, 108
command: 35, 41, 43, 56, 79, 82, 95
Command-Query Responsibility Segregation: 47
Command-Query Separation: 47
compiler: 40-41, 117, 122
component: 4-6, 11-13, 15, 28, 102-107, 109-110
contracts: 60, 64, 72
controller: 27-28, 53, 55-56, 82, 92, 104
coupling: 3, 16, 128
CRUD: 68, 91, 93, 94, 131, 132

D

DDD: 16, 26, 31, 44, 64, 96, 136
debugging: 94
decoupling: 16
delegate: 72

dependency: 11-15, 17-18, 22, 26-28, 50, 59-60, 62, 101-103, 105, 107, 109, 115-117, 119-122, 129-130
dependency injection: 18, 28, 101, 103, 105, 115, 116
dependency inversion principle: 11, 13, 22, 27, 50, 60, 121
dependency rule: 15, 17, 102, 115, 117, 119, 120
domain: 1-3, 5-7, 13-18, 22-27, 31-32, 34, 36, 42-45, 47, 52-53, 57, 60-61, 64-66, 71-72, 77-78, 84, 87-89, 91-96, 101, 115-119, 121, 129-132, 136-137
Domain-Driven Design: 16, 96, 136
domain layer: 2, 3, 5, 7, 13, 14, 16, 23, 93, 117
domain model: 16, 25, 26, 31, 32, 42, 44, 66, 71, 72, 92, 93, 94, 95, 96, 132
domain-specific language: 87, 118

E

end-to-end: 77
entities: 2, 3, 4, 15, 16, 17, 18, 24, 34, 43, 44, 45, 47, 61, 69, 77, 78, 121, 129
entity: 5, 14, 16, 31-34, 42-45, 53, 61-62, 65-67, 71, 77-78, 82, 88, 129-130, 132
erosion: 113

errors: 40, 62, 84, 107, 120, 122

F

facade: 21
factory: 39, 66, 96, 108
framework: 3, 16, 28, 61, 82, 87, 92, 94, 101, 103, 105, 107, 109, 117

G

generic: 4, 94, 115
GitHub: 117, 119
Gradle: 119, 122

H

hardware: 125
hexagon: 17, 38
hexagonal architecture: 11, 16, 17, 18, 21, 24, 25, 27, 30, 31, 38, 60, 75, 76, 77, 87, 88, 89, 129, 136, 137
hierarchy: 53

I

incoming adapter: 25, 27, 34, 50, 51, 52, 95, 121, 130, 131, 132
incoming port: 25, 26, 27, 36, 38, 46, 47, 50, 51, 65, 94, 115, 121, 129, 130, 131
input model: 37, 39, 40, 41, 42, 52, 61, 95, 96, 128, 130, 132
integration test: 76, 77, 80, 82, 87, 88, 89

Interface Segregation Principle: 11, 62, 63
immutable: 38, 40-41, 66
import: 21, 82, 84
inherited: 13
initialize: 40
injection: 18, 26, 28, 101, 103, 105, 115-116
in-memory: 84-85
interface: 11, 14, 17-18, 22, 24-25, 27-28, 36, 49, 61-63, 68-69, 76-77, 89, 92, 95-97, 102, 106, 129-130
isolated: 102, 110, 120, 122

J

Java Config: 107
JPA: 3, 61, 64, 65, 67, 68, 69, 71, 109

L

library: 13, 80, 106

M

mapper: 91, 108
mapping: 3, 16, 42, 61, 71, 82, 84, 87, 91-98, 121
Maven: 119, 122
Mockito: 80
model-code gap: 25
models: 41-42, 45, 47, 56, 61, 71, 91-92, 94-97, 127-129
modifiers: 115-116
modules: 109-110, 115, 117, 120-123
monolithic: 119

O

object-relational mapping: 3, 16, 61
one-way: 96-97
OR-Mapper: 64
outgoing adapter: 25, 26, 27, 34, 35, 51, 60, 121, 130, 131, 132
outgoing port: 23, 24, 25, 26, 27, 36, 45, 47, 51, 62, 63, 94, 96, 98, 102, 115, 121, 130
output model: 45, 47, 61, 92, 95, 96, 127, 128, 129, 130

P

persistence adapter: 23, 25, 27, 28, 34, 59, 60, 61, 63, 64, 65, 68, 69, 71, 72, 82, 84, 87, 101, 102, 103, 104, 105, 106, 107, 108, 109, 116, 117, 120, 131
persistence layer: 2, 3, 4, 5, 6, 7, 13, 14, 16, 31, 59, 60, 61, 634, 71, 72, 91, 92, 93, 94, 95, 97, 98, 109, 121
port: 17, 18, 23, 24, 25, 26, 27, 34, 36, 38, 45, 46, 47, 50, 51, 60, 61, 62, 63, 64, 65, 69, 71, 86, 87, 89, 94. 95. 96. 98, 102, 115, 116, 121, 129, 130, 131

R

read-only: 46-47, 97
refactor: 80, 107
repository: 14, 62,
    68-69, 108, 119, 122

S

semantical: 42
server: 103
setter: 44
shortcut: 4, 8, 45, 47,
    51, 125, 126, 127,
    128, 130, 132, 135
Single Responsibility
    Principle: 11, 45, 92,
    94, 103, 121, 122, 128
Spring: 65, 67, 68, 69, 72,
    82, 84, 85, 86, 101, 105,
    106, 107, 108, 109, 116
Spring Boot: 69, 82,
    101, 108, 109
Spring Data: 65, 67,
    69, 84, 108
stateless: 80
system test: 76,
    77, 85, 87, 88

T

transactional: 35, 43, 72

U

unit tests: 76, 77,
    78, 79, 82, 89
use case: 5, 6, 7, 8, 15, 17,
    21, 22, 23, 28, 31, 32, 34,
    35, 36, 37, 38, 41, 42,
    43, 44, 45, 46, 47, 50,
    51, 52, 53, 55, 56, 57,
    64, 65, 72, 77, 78, 80,
    82, 85, 87, 88, 91, 92,
    93, 94, 95, 97, 98, 101,
    102, 103, 104, 115, 121,
    127, 128, 129, 130, 131
utility: 4

V

validation: 34, 36, 37, 38,
    39, 40, 41, 42, 44, 47, 52,
    66, 80, 82, 93, 95, 97
violation: 39, 117, 122, 126

W

web adapter: 17, 23, 27,
    28, 49, 50, 51, 52, 53,
    54, 57, 81, 80, 82, 87,
    101, 103, 104, 109, 120
web layer: 1, 2, 3, 5, 6, 7,
    53, 92, 94, 95, 97, 121

CPSIA information can be obtained
at www.ICGtesting.com
Printed in the USA
LVHW061349180422
716527LV00020B/259